Free Jazz

SUNY Press Jazz Styles

Free Jazz

JEFF SCHWARTZ

Published by State University of New York Press, Albany

© 2022 State University of New York

All rights reserved

Printed in the United States of America

No part of this book may be used or reproduced in any manner whatsoever without written permission. No part of this book may be stored in a retrieval system or transmitted in any form or by any means including electronic, electrostatic, magnetic tape, mechanical, photocopying, recording, or otherwise without the prior permission in writing of the publisher.

For information, contact State University of New York Press, Albany, NY
www.sunypress.edu

Library of Congress Cataloging-in-Publication Data

Name: Schwartz, Jeff, author.
Title: Free jazz / Jeff Schwartz.
Description: Albany : State University of New York Press, 2022. | Series: SUNY Press jazz styles | Includes bibliographical references and index.
Identifiers: LCCN 2022002679 (print) | LCCN 2022002680 (ebook) | ISBN 9781438490311 (hardcover : alk. paper) | ISBN 9781438490328 (ebook) | ISBN 9781438490304 (pbk. : alk. paper)
Subjects: LCSH: Free jazz—History and criticism.
Classification: LCC ML3506 .S38515 2022 (print) | LCC ML3506 (ebook) | DDC 781.65/6—dc23
LC record available at https://lccn.loc.gov/2022002679
LC ebook record available at https://lccn.loc.gov/2022002680

10 9 8 7 6 5 4 3 2 1

Contents

Acknowledgments	vii
Introduction	1
Chapter Overviews	5
1. Freedom	11
Free	20
Harmolodics	21
Time, No Changes	24
2. Spirituality	31
A Love Supreme	35
Universal Consciousness	37
The Nubians of Plutonia	38
New Africa	40
Karma	42
Bridge into the New Age	44
3. Energy	51
Ascension	58
Machine Gun	60
We Now Create	66
4. Experimentalism	67
Imaginary Values	68
Sound Structure of Subculture Becoming	70
Ankhrasmation	73

Language Music	76
Zooid	83
Conduction	85
Search and Reflect	91
5. Self-determination	95
The Jazz Composers Guild	96
Self-Reliance Productions	101
Wildflowers	104
Uptown and Downtown	111
6. Ancient to the Future	115
A Jackson in Your House	115
Dogon A.D.	120
Notes	127
Index	153

Acknowledgments

Thanks first to my editor Richard Carlin. This book was written in response to a call he posted on the Jazz Studies Collaborative Facebook group. That group, the Improvisation Studies section of the Society for Ethnomusicology, Ben Young's *From the Lab* radio show and Zoom session, and the Popular Music Books in Process series organized through the *Journal of Popular Music Studies*, the Pop Conference, and the US chapter of the International Association for the Study of Popular Music have been valuable sources of guidance, community, and inspiration during the COVID-19 pandemic.

Many thanks to the musicians, journalists, critics, academics, and others whose work I have drawn on. I hope my notes will lead readers to these original sources. I am also grateful to the scholars, performers, and friends who have provided more direct feedback and support: Andrew Apter, Kyle Barnett, Andrea Centazzo, Jack Curtis Dubowsky, Jonathon Grasse, Ras Moshe, Anne Rhodes, Charles Sharp, Sean Sonderegger, Carl Testa, and Kenny Wessel.

Thanks to Jessica Catron, Jeremy Drake, and David Rothbaum (line space line), François Houle (Vancouver Creative Music Institute), Michelle Yom (Unit Structures Conference), Karl Berger, Ingrid Sersto, Rob Saffer, Steven Bernstein, and Billy Martin (Creative Music Studio), Nina Eidsheim and Steven Loza (UCLA), Alex Cline and Will Salmon (Open Gate), and Lisa Mezzacappa and Jason Levis (dBxB Experimental Band), for creating situations where I could meet, play with, and learn from artists including Steve Adams, Karen Borca, Bobby Bradford, Anthony Braxton, Ellen Burr, John Butcher, Taylor Ho Bynum, Dan Clucas, Marilyn Crispell, Marty Ehrlich, Ken Filiano, Wolfgang Fuchs, Vinny Golia, Mats Gustafsson, Barry Guy, Mary Halvorson, Mark Helias, Wayne Horvitz,

Jason Kao Hwang, Vijay Iyer, Lynn Johnston, Kirk Knuffke, Oliver Lake, Joëlle Léandre, Anne LeBaron, Elliott Levin, James Brandon Lewis, Steuart Liebig, André Martinez, Nicole Mitchell, Evan Parker, Garth Powell, Jon Raskin, Dana Reason, Gino Robair, Rent Romus, William Roper, Sara Schoenbeck, Wadada Leo Smith, Warren Smith, Tyshawn Sorey, Raymond Strid, Henry Threadgill, Peter Valsamis, Fay Victor, and Rich West. Thanks to them for sharing their music and insight.

Finally, my deepest appreciation to my brother Jay Schwartz for his patent and generous reading of my drafts, and my love to my wife Leah Pressman.

Introduction

The short version of the story of free jazz is that in 1959 Ornette Coleman came to New York playing music that did not use preset structures for improvising. This influenced established musicians from his generation including John Coltrane, Charles Mingus, Sonny Rollins, and Miles Davis, and inspired younger players to explore new approaches, initially in New York, then in Chicago, St. Louis, Los Angeles, Europe, South Africa, Japan, and worldwide. Musicians organized their own performance venues, record labels, and cooperative organizations to control, support, and present their own work. This drive for creative freedom and economic self-determination paralleled the radical politics of the 1960s, especially the African-American civil rights and Black Power movements.

This version is basically true, but it does not address this music's diversity, complexity, or endurance. It doesn't mention the musicians exploring similar areas before or alongside Coleman and understates the amount of structure and composition in his music and in free jazz in general. It also risks limiting free jazz to the 1960s and early 1970s, as one might think of bebop as a music of the 1940s and 1950s or disco the 1970s, while vital work continues to be made both by free jazz artists from the 1960s, such as Marshall Allen, Barry Altschul, Han Bennink, Karl Berger, Carla Bley, Bobby Bradford, Anthony Braxton, Peter Brötzmann, Andrew Cyrille, Barry Guy, Dave Holland, Roscoe Mitchell, Evan Parker, Pharoah Sanders, Archie Shepp, Alan Silva, Wadada Leo Smith, Henry Threadgill, Trevor Watts, and Reggie Workman, and by subsequent generations.

The innovations of free jazz can mostly be understood as alternatives to song form, which had previously defined a common practice. Although a wide variety of variations and complications were possible, a jazz performance essentially consisted of a melodic theme, followed by improvised solos on the form of the theme, then a concluding restatement of the theme. The rhythm section repeated the chord progression of the theme throughout while soloists invented new melodies that fit those harmonies. The twelve-bar blues is the most essential of these forms, while other themes and their forms largely came from Tin Pan Alley and Broadway. Jazz grew up alongside these popular music institutions from the 1920s to the 1960s, and the canon of jazz standards overlaps substantially with the American Songbook of composers such as George Gershwin, Cole Porter, and Richard Rodgers. Jazz soloists from Louis Armstrong to John Coltrane developed their styles to navigate the harmonies common in this music, and jazz composers of this era, whether Duke Ellington or Horace Silver, wrote essentially in song form using a combination of blues and show-tune harmony.

This common practice enabled musicians to collaborate with minimal preparation and has facilitated such intergenerational and polystylistic teams as John Coltrane and Duke Ellington, Sonny Rollins and Coleman Hawkins, John Zorn and Big John Patton, and various Jazz at the Philharmonic lineups. At the 1958 Newport Jazz Festival bassist Henry Grimes played in bands led by Benny Goodman, Lee Konitz, Thelonious Monk, Gerry Mulligan, Sonny Rollins, and Tony Scott, an extraordinary feat, possible in part because these groups, and every other at the festival, were grounded in a common practice. These artists had different composing and soloing styles, but they all played over cyclic song forms using familiar chord progressions outlined by swinging walking bass lines.

There is plenty of free jazz that uses song forms. For example, Archie Shepp's "Mama Too Tight" is a funky blues that easily could have been recorded by Lee Morgan or James Brown's bands, and David Murray's "Flowers for Albert" is a thirty-two-bar AABA song using standard harmonies. These tunes are free jazz because of the choices the soloists make and because Shepp and Murray's careers have unfolded in what sociologists would call the "art world" of free jazz.[1] The musicians they work with, labels they record for, venues they play, magazines and websites that cover them, and so on, are all connected to free jazz.

However, this book will focus on the alternatives to song form introduced through free jazz. Composer/bassist Charles Mingus, pianist Paul Bley, and composer/author Gunther Schuller all observed in the 1950s that, although bebop musicians were stretching tonality in their composed and improvised melodies, they remained tethered to popular song harmonies. In his 1957 essay "The Future of Form in Jazz," Schuller listed a dozen compositional innovators, highlighting Mingus and Jimmy Giuffre in particular, but concluded that the music was waiting for a "new Charlie Parker" to introduce the next style after bebop. Bley, who worked with Parker, Mingus, Giuffre, and Ornette Coleman, among others, makes the same observations in his memoir, and both he and Schuller claim Coleman became that "new Charlie Parker."[2]

Trumpet player and composer Bill Dixon, organizer of the 1964 October Revolution, the first free jazz festival, argued that the "revolution" was moving from a song form–based common practice to a constellation of idiosyncratic musical concepts associated with individual artists. Like Mingus, Schuller, and Bley, he saw these new approaches as exploring implications of bebop without the underlying structures borrowed from popular music.[3]

There were experiments with free improvisation by modernists, including some of the players listed by Schuller and Bley, such as Lennie Tristano's "Intuition" and "Digression" in 1949, Shelly Manne's "Abstract #1" from 1954 with Jimmy Giuffre and Shorty Rogers, Chico Hamilton's 1955 "Free Form," Mingus's "Getting Together" and "Gregarian Chant," and an unreleased series of 1957 workshop sessions where composer Edgard Varèse directed a group that included Mingus.[4] However, none of these led to free playing becoming a major element of any artist's approach or a recognized jazz style.

"Free jazz" did not become a genre name until the late 1960s. Terms like "the New Thing," the avant-garde, playing "out," "outside," "free," or "freeform" circulated, and Amiri Baraka (then known as LeRoi Jones), one of the music's main critical advocates, tried to popularize "New Black Music," but Ornette Coleman's 1961 album *Free Jazz* eventually lent its name to the movement.[5] Coleman, like many free jazz artists, attempted to reject the term. He claimed the album was named by his record company, that he never liked the title, and that it did not reflect how he understood his music.[6] Pianist Marilyn Crispell has said she "hates" the label, and many other artists such as Julius Hemphill, Misha Mengelberg, and Anthony Braxton have similarly disavowed it.[7] According to George Lewis, the members of Chicago's Association for the Advancement of Creative Musicians (AACM) cooperative almost never referred to their music as "free jazz."[8]

Lewis has also argued that the music of the AACM and their peers should not be considered jazz at all, and that doing so can be a musical version of the racist "one-drop" rule under which one African-American ancestor made a person legally Black. He observes that Black experimentalists such as Anthony Braxton, Muhal Richard Abrams, Anthony Davis, and himself are frequently described and judged as jazz musicians, no matter what their music is like, while white experimentalists such as Earle Brown, LaMonte Young, Derek Bailey, John Zorn, and Keith Rowe are assumed to have transcended their backgrounds in jazz, even when their work includes improvisation, propulsive rhythms, or other qualities commonly associated with jazz.[9] Applying a prescriptive or traditionalist definition of jazz, such as Stanley Crouch's "swing, blues, ballads, and the Spanish tinge," to much of the music called free jazz will find it wanting, just as a search for those elements in the music of LaMonte Young or Keith Rowe will fail. Describing Lewis as a "jazz composer" rather than as a composer who sometimes writes and plays jazz presumes both that, like Crouch, we know what jazz is, and that we know Lewis is part of it. It narrowly defines the genre, assigns artists to it, and judges them by that definition, ignoring their intentions or the manifest characteristics of their work.

However, Lewis also describes "jazz" as a "social location within which sound and musical practice take on additional meanings."[10] Free jazz artists have occupied this location, voluntarily or not, and some have claimed the jazz tradition as one of ongoing exploration, a "perpetual frontier," as guitarist Joe Morris entitled his book.[11] The label can be understood to authorize creativity rather than confine it, although it still carries racial and cultural hierarchy.

This study will try to avoid Crouch-like essential definitions of jazz or free jazz but to consider artists and works on their own terms. This means pieces such as Anthony Braxton's "Composition 76" and Wadada Leo Smith's "The Bell" will be discussed as examples of new compositional and improvisational options opened by free jazz. They would not exist if there was no free jazz, but whether or not they are themselves jazz or free jazz will be left to the listener.

Saxophonist Ken Vandermark has argued that free jazz lasted from Ornette Coleman's 1959 New York debut to John Coltrane's death in 1967. Of course, many artists associated with free jazz continued making work after 1967, and new ones, including Vandermark himself, have emerged since. His claim is that after 1967 free jazz had become a knowable style, and that after the late 1960s musicians often used the techniques associated with Coleman, Coltrane, and other first-generation free jazz players such as Cecil Taylor and Albert Ayler alongside other elements.[12] This study is grounded in the period defined by Vandermark but will follow artists and ideas to the present. One model for this is Thomas Owens's *Bebop: The Music and Its Players*, which traces the dissemination of musical elements introduced in the 1940s into the 1990s.[13]

Rather than a move away from central free jazz musical practices, the genre and style-crossing work made after 1967 by Sun Ra, Archie Shepp, the Art Ensemble of Chicago, Don Cherry, the Instant Composers Pool, and many others represents the freedom to explore a variety of materials and systems: free jazz as a metamusic. Free jazz is not inherently or essentially freeform; there are free jazz pieces that are completely written out, as well as those that are entirely improvised, and everything in-between. It is not a single identifiable style but includes multiple expansions of the form and language of jazz. Joe Morris described this as "freedom to" do new things rather than "freedom from" old things, and Amiri Baraka wrote that the "free" in "free jazz" is a verb, not an adjective.[14]

Chapter Overviews

The key earlier overviews of free jazz—Val Wilmer's *As Serious as Your Life*, John Litweiler's *The Freedom Principle*, and Ekkehard Jost's *Free Jazz*—are all organized chronologically and focused on a core group of major artists. Wilmer was a music journalist and photographer; her book relies on her firsthand experiences in New York and England and interviews she conducted in the 1960s and 1970s. Litweiler similarly built his career as a jazz journalist as one of the first to cover the AACM in the 1960s, while Jost's book is primarily technical musical analysis.[15]

This book takes a different approach. Each chapter covers one formal and aesthetic area opened by free jazz: new ways that people started playing music and why. These are not necessarily subgenres or schools of free jazz playing; few pieces or artists will fall neatly into one chapter. Instead, these are some of the things that were new about the music called the New Thing. Examples are often chosen because they help illustrate these things, not because they were the first or are the best. The artists and pieces discussed represent sources and limits of these formal and aesthetic innovations, not a canon of free jazz. There is no discography or recommended listening list at the end of this book. The goal is to suggest things to listen for rather than what to listen to.

Chapter 1 is on "time, no changes" playing: music that keeps the texture and feeling of bebop but suspends or eliminates chord changes or song form, introduced on the series of extremely influential albums Ornette Coleman made for Atlantic Records between 1959 and 1961. In this period of Coleman's music, during both the themes and solos, the horns often play angular eighth note lines while the bass walks and the drums play swinging time, as in bebop. Sometimes the ensemble maintains a regular form without allowing it to dictate what is played. Coleman in particular seems to pour improvised melody into space rather than connecting harmonic landmarks. They also play compositions where, after the initial melody, the bass and drums play time without a set form, choosing pitches and defining phrases spontaneously in relation to the soloist. This approach was adopted by numerous free jazz groups as well as by bands not often considered part of the movement, such as Miles Davis's Second Great Quintet and Keith Jarrett's American Quartet.

Chapter 2 is on what has become known as spiritual jazz, a term popularized by writers, fans, record collectors, DJs, and concert presenters to describe some of the music growing out of John Coltrane's work between 1960 and 1965. Coltrane's hit 1960 adaptation of "My Favorite Things" from *The Sound of Music* suggested both India, by reducing the harmonic movement to a cued change of mode on the same tonic, and Africa, by replacing the original straight waltz feel with a three-over-two polyrhythm. Subsequent pieces, including "Olé," "Africa," and "India" (all recorded in 1961), explicitly connected modal improvisation with exotic settings, while those such as "Spiritual" (1961), "Alabama" (1963), *A Love Supreme* (1964), and *Om* (1965) increasingly approached music as a religious practice. This was at odds with jazz's association with nightlife but suited the spiritual explorations of the emerging counterculture. After John Coltrane's death in 1967, his bandmates Pharoah Sanders and Alice Coltrane (also his widow) became leading exponents of this style. Their work often used repeated bass lines outlining simple chord progressions and found affinities in psychedelic and progressive rock, rhythm and blues, and early jazz/rock.

Chapter 3 covers energy music, exemplified by Albert Ayler's 1965 piece "Holy Ghost," with Sunny Murray on drums. Murray and other free jazz drummers moved away from playing countable time, marking beats or bar lines, or expressing other expected rhythmic elements. The music is propelled instead by waves of intensity, with each player keeping their contribution moving ahead on its own and in relation to others' rather than to a rhythmic pulse or grid. This can sound like everyone is soloing at once, and there is often a maximalist sensibility in energy music: louder, higher, faster. German bassist Peter Kowald used the term *"kaputtspiel"* to describe a music that seeks to "tear apart the old values" through sheer sonic force, but players and critics also associated the force of this music with spiritual ecstasy.[16] Mid-to-late 1960s recordings such as John Coltrane's *Ascension*, Peter Brötzmann's *Machine Gun*, and Mashiko Togashi's *We Now Create* illustrate some of the expressive range of energy music: religious possession, political militancy, and defiant assertion of identity.

Chapter 4 addresses experimentalism. This includes completely improvised music, which interprets the freedom of free jazz as freedom from any precomposed material or predetermined structures. Sam Rivers's groups of the 1970 embraced episodes of harmonic stability, rhythmic groove, and references to other musical styles during their improvised sets, while others, especially the network of British groups around the Little Theatre Club, rigorously avoided these elements.

Freedom from established systems, forms, and values also permitted artists to explore new ways of structuring performances, including graphic and text notation, alternative systems of pitch and rhythmic organization, conducting and cuing techniques, and unorthodox uses of conventionally scored material. Examples of these approaches are drawn from the work of Cecil Taylor, Wadada Leo Smith, Anthony Braxton, Henry Threadgill, Lawrence "Butch" Morris, and John Stevens.

The politics and economics of free jazz are considered in chapter 5. Writing in the first half of the 1960s, Amiri Baraka called Sonny Rollins and John Coltrane "assassins" out to "completely destroy the popular song."[17] He and other critics aligned free jazz with other liberation and self-determination movements. Leaving song form meant leaving American mass culture and the culture industry to create an autonomous art music without vestigial Tin Pan Alley and Broadway material. Many artists also sought control of their recordings and live performances. Independent and artist-run record labels and performance venues multiplied both out of necessity, as commercial platforms turned away from this music, and as alternatives to white supremacist cultural and economic systems. Free jazz was a significant element of the Black Arts Movement of the mid-1960s to 1970s. Many free jazz musicians also pursued alternative ways to produce and present work, because, unlike the classical avant-garde, this music developed largely without academic, foundation, or government support.[18] Some solutions, such as staging performances in lofts and other nontraditional spaces and developing new networks for booking shows and distributing self-produced recordings, were models for subsequent underground and DIY music scenes.[19] More recently, free jazz artists have received major grants, awards, and academic appointments.

The conclusion is entitled "Ancient to the Future," after the motto of the AACM. It considers free jazz's role in jazz history through two pieces: the Art Ensemble of Chicago's 1969 recording of saxophonist Roscoe Mitchell's "A Jackson in Your House" and Julius Hemphill's 1972 "Dogon A.D." The first represents free jazz incorporating the existing history of jazz, with self-aware references to past styles and materials, while the second represents the innovations of free jazz becoming part of a new common practice.

"A Jackson in Your House" is a short tonal melody. The band plays it several times, sometimes pausing for spoken passages and sound effects. Each repetition uses a different combination of interpretive and improvisational approaches, from quasi-classical to New Orleans to a section featuring metal chimes, bells, and bowls. Here the freedom of free jazz includes the freedom to play in or with historical styles. While improvisers like Charlie Parker and Dexter Gordon regularly quoted phrases from classical warhorses and popular songs in their solos, it was quite rare for jazz musicians to make substantial historical and stylistic references in their work. The other half of the AACM's motto is "Great Black Music"; their references are about claiming a history and a context as well as commenting on the past. Like Archie Shepp's late 1960s albums *The Cry of My People* and *Attica Blues*, Carla Bley's *Escalator Over the Hill*, Sun Ra's performances, and Don Cherry's work on albums including *Mu*, *Eternal Rhythm*, *Relativity Suite*, and *Actions*, the Art Ensemble often presented a panoply of musical forms, genres, and styles in the context of free jazz.[20]

Saxophonist Julius Hemphill's "Dogon A.D." alternates funky and angular melodic phrases over an odd-meter blues riff. The title refers to the West African Dogon people, and "A.D." their adapted dance, which revised ceremonial movements into formats more suitable for tourists by borrowing from European dance and by intentionally suppressing their most profound elements. Hemphill first recorded it in 1972, with a rough-edged quartet from St. Louis's Black Artists Group, including trumpet, cello, and drums.[21] He returned to it in 1984, on the LP *Georgia Blue*, joined by percussionist Jumma Santos and three young white musicians from Los Angeles: bass guitarist Steuart Liebig and twin brothers Alex and Nels Cline on drums and guitar, respectively. They had absorbed John

Coltrane and the Art Ensemble alongside Jimi Hendrix, Frank Zappa, and the Mahavishnu Orchestra and brought techniques and technologies of progressive and psychedelic rock to Hemphill's music. In 2009, Vijay Iyer released a version of "Dogon A.D." by his piano trio, whose repertoire included many odd-meter vamp pieces related to Indian music, and another cover appeared in 2019 by the free jazz repertory ensemble Broken Shadows, which combines saxophonists Tim Berne (a student of Hemphill's) and Chris Speed with the bassist and drummer from the Bad Plus, a piano trio whose notorious adaptations of songs by Black Sabbath and Nirvana helped build an audience for their rock-influenced original music.

These and several other versions of "Dogon A.D." suggest how ideas from free jazz have become part of a hybridized contemporary jazz mainstream. Artists like Nels Cline, Vijay Iyer, Tim Berne, Chris Speed, and the Bad Plus, as well as Ambrose Akinmusire, Dave Douglas, Kamasi Washington, Joe Lovano, Chris Potter, Mark Turner, Jason Moran, Craig Taborn, Matt Mitchell, Eric Revis, Dave Holland, Myra Melford, Dan Weiss, Tyshawn Sorey, Mary Halvorson, Bill Frisell, Ken Vandermark, Miguel Zenón, Nicole Mitchell, Joe Morris, Kris Davis, Steve Lehman, Rudresh Mahanthappa, Matana Roberts, Marc Ribot, Medeski, Martin, and Wood, John Zorn, and many others now regularly headline festivals and win awards with work that mixes traditional jazz practices with the expanded options associated with free jazz, including elements of non-Western music and contemporary classical composition as well as aspects of hip-hop, rock, and other popular genres.

1

Freedom

Historian Fred Kaplan and musician Darius Brubeck both call 1959 a pivotal year in jazz, listing classic albums recorded that year, including Miles Davis's *Kind of Blue*, Charles Mingus's *Mingus Ah Um*, and *Time Out* by Darius's father Dave. Brubeck also argues that increased publication of jazz instructional materials, record labels anthologizing and reissuing older recordings, and formalization of jazz education at the end of the 1950s represented a growing artistic, theoretical, and historical self-consciousness.[1] Looking at some 1959 albums, including popular hits and canonical masterpieces covered by Kaplan and Brubeck, as well as more obscure titles, will show some of the creative currents running into free jazz.

Kind of Blue, recorded in March and April, consists of five Davis compositions. "All Blues" and "Freddie Freeloader" are blues. "Blue in Green" is a short ballad, almost certainly actually written by pianist Bill Evans. "So What" and "Flamenco Sketches" have more unusual forms, but all the pieces are medium to slow tempo and have simple melodies, eschewing the angularity and unpredictability of bebop. This album was the culmination of Davis's interest in slowing down and smoothing out harmonic movement in order to explore the sounds of individual scales. "So What" is a thirty-two-bar AABA song form, but it has no chord changes. Instead, the A section uses the D Dorian mode, the white keys of the piano from D to D, and the B section is the same scale a half step higher. In both the horn figures and piano accompaniment, these modes are harmonized in fourths, which avoids creating the tensions and resolutions of standard triadic harmony. "Flamenco Sketches" sets song form aside entirely; the improvisation is based on a series of scales that change on cue from the soloist. They move in sequence, but the length of each is not predetermined. Gunther Schuller featured Mingus's earlier uses of this unusual type of structure in "The Future of Form in Jazz."[2]

Kind of Blue has become one of the most popular and revered albums in jazz. The music it inspired has become known as "modal jazz," but, while compositions such as "So What" are modally based, the improvisers do not limit themselves to those scales as musicians in the modal traditions of India, Iran, or the Arab world would. Instead, as jazz musicians, Davis, Evans, John Coltrane, and Cannonball Adderley bring their full vocabulary of chromaticism, harmonic superimpositions, and blues elements to these tunes.[3] However, grounding these improvisations in scales rather than cyclic harmony presented an alternative to song form.

"Take Five," the hit Paul Desmond composition from Dave Brubeck's *Time Out*, recorded in the summer of 1959 and released in December, also suggested modal jazz. While it is a thirty-two-bar AABA form, the A section is a repeated one-bar figure alternating two chords. Only the bridge moves harmonically. This formula of a riff-based A section and cyclic chord changes in the bridge is common in Latin jazz tunes such as Dizzy Gillespie's "Manteca" and "A Night in Tunisia." Brubeck also popularized meters beyond the three- and four-beat patterns typical of American popular music, such as the 5/4 of "Take Five." He specifically linked many of these to "world music" sources, mostly Eastern Europe and the Near East, such as "Blue Rondo a la Turk," which is in a Turkish seven-beat rhythm.

At almost the same time that he collaborated with Miles Davis on *Kind of Blue*, which seemed to ask how few notes or chords a jazz composition needed, John Coltrane experimented with maximizing harmonic movement in the title track and "Countdown" from his album *Giant Steps*, recorded in March and May. Each of these has a chord change every two or four beats and was played at a lightning tempo of over 280 beats per minute, so Coltrane and his band were dealing with around two chords every second. As Eric Nisenson writes, these pieces seemed to take the challenge of playing complex chord changes at fast tempos to "a final extreme."[4] Guitarist John Schott has observed that the rapid symmetrical chord movement in "Giant Steps" leads Coltrane to use all twelve pitches almost equally. His solo is very consonant, in that his notes closely fit the chords, but it is also atonal, because the fast symmetrical rotation of pitches and movement through key centers denies the drama of leaving and returning to a home key. Like Nisenson, Schott concludes, "Coltrane destroyed tonality by using it against itself."[5]

Cecil Taylor's 1959 album *Love for Sale* raised similar questions about tonality and form. It contains three Cole Porter compositions and three Taylor originals, all in song forms, but these forms often sound on the verge of falling apart. The bass and drums do not always agree on the tempo or groove and sometimes one will drop out, possibly to reset. These would be serious flaws in a conventional performance but happen frequently enough to appear intentional. Instead of a stable backup, the rhythm section is a zone of creative contention.

Taylor's piano playing is full of clusters: groups of adjacent pitches. These sometimes are percussive accents, such as Horace Silver or Thelonious Monk would use, but at other times they seem to be challenges to the musical structure, either by taking harmonic extensions that would work in a bebop melody and stacking them into dense chords or by juxtaposing atonal material with the harmonic form maintained by the bass. Taylor knows what song the band is playing, where they are in the form, and what the chord changes are, but he chooses to not express these things as clearly or consistently as his contemporaries.[6]

Something structurally similar but aesthetically quite different often happens on Bill Evans's *Portrait in Jazz*, recorded in December. *Kind of Blue* was Evans's last session with Davis; he subsequently worked almost exclusively as a leader and *Portrait in Jazz* was the debut of his best-known group, a trio with bassist Scott LaFaro and drummer Paul Motian. They established a style of playing that Evans's subsequent trios continued: while they played song forms, they approached them obliquely, as if they knew them so well that it was unnecessary and maybe even unsophisticated to mark the chord changes, sectional divisions, and even downbeats too clearly. Although LaFaro played straight walking bass in other contexts, with Evans he frequently interrupted his line with other figures or improvised melodically. He and Motian often seem to play in relation to the form rather than directly playing the form. While Evans was not a free jazz player, some of his band members such as LaFaro, Motian, Gary Peacock, and Eddie Gomez did notable work in free jazz, and the independence and interaction in Evans's bands set a precedent.

By demonstrating how drummers and bassists could play around song form, Evans's rhythm sections implied how they could play without it.[7]

Jimmy Giuffre recorded two compositions for his clarinet and an orchestral string section in Germany in March 1959. Each filled one side of the LP *Piece for Clarinet and String Orchestra/Mobiles*, and both use a similar harmonic palette, showing Giuffre's studies of his contemporaries in the classical world, such as Stravinsky and Copland, as well as those composers' debts to jazz. However, they are significantly different structurally: "Piece for Clarinet and String Orchestra" contains no improvisation, while the solo clarinet part in "Mobiles" is entirely improvised. "Mobiles" also includes several unaccompanied clarinet interludes, and there are sections in the string parts where the choice of rhythms is left to the players or the conductor spontaneously cues the duration, articulation, orchestration, repetition, and volume of chords. Ordinarily a conductor steers the interpretation of an already fully written work, but Giuffre delegated the power to determine major details in real time, not simply the precise tempo of the "presto" movement, but which notes will be played by which instruments, how loudly, how many times, and so on.[8] Composers such as John Cage, Morton Feldman, and Pierre Boulez were working with similar open form scores and improvisational conducting in the European-American experimental music scene at this time. In particular Earle Brown, who had some experience in jazz, and Lukas Foss with his Improvisation Chamber Ensemble required conductors to make spontaneous decisions as Giuffre did.[9] Conducted improvisation became a recognized part of the jazz language through free jazz, as did completely free improvisation and unaccompanied solo playing, techniques all represented in "Mobiles."

Ornette Coleman recorded three albums in 1959 and made his New York debut on November 17 at the Five Spot. Although the term "free jazz" was not yet in use, Coleman was received as introducing a new jazz style, with substantial press coverage pro and con, including assessments from musicians ranging from Lionel Hampton to Leonard Bernstein. This attention was largely generated through the advocacy of Modern Jazz Quartet pianist John Lewis and jazz critics Martin Williams and Gunther Schuller. Lewis heard Coleman while the MJQ was in Los Angeles in 1958 and brought him to the 1959 session of the Lenox School of Jazz to present his work to the faculty of critics and musicians, including Williams, Schuller, Jimmy Giuffre, and George Russell. Impressed, Williams then secured the November Five Spot booking.[10]

Coleman's first album, *Something Else!*, appeared in November 1958, followed by *Tomorrow Is the Question* a year later. On these records, made for the Los Angeles independent label Contemporary, the label insisted that Coleman and trumpet player Don Cherry use well-known rhythm section players, including Shelly Manne, Red Mitchell, and MJQ bassist Percy Heath. When Coleman switched to the major label Atlantic, through Lewis, Williams, and Schuller's support, he was able to use his working band: Cherry, bassist Charlie Haden, and drummer Billy Higgins, who were more familiar with his approach. They recorded *The Shape of Jazz to Come* in May 1959 for a November release and *Change of the Century* in October to appear in May 1960. Coleman and this quartet moved from LA to New York between the *Change of the Century* session and the Five Spot shows. Since there are no recordings from the Five Spot, these albums are the closest thing to a document of what those audiences heard.

Amazingly, over sixty years later, there continues to be significant disagreement about not just the merits of this music but also its essential formal properties. Astute and credible listeners have claimed both that the solos on these records have no preset form and that they follow song forms, whether the sometimes irregular ones of Coleman's themes or standard twelve-bar blues and thirty-two-bar rhythm changes.[11] Analyzing these various understandings will help show what Coleman's music has meant, how it works, and why it matters.

One source of confusion is Coleman himself. A self-taught musician and organic intellectual, he habitually used technical musical terms with personal abstract meanings. The many interviews he gave and the handful of texts he published are fascinating, but they answer few specific questions about his music.[12] Coleman largely bypassed even the informal education many jazz musicians received through apprenticeships with established artists. His music career up to 1958 consisted of work with blues bands and a minstrel show in Texas and playing in jazz jam sessions around Los Angeles, all with mixed results.[13] He had few opportunities to learn how professional jazz musicians thought and talked about their music, which contributed to his idiosyncratic discourse.[14]

His advocates celebrated what they perceived as his spontaneity and primitivism. Gunther Schuller wrote, "Perhaps the most outstanding element in Ornette's musical conception is an utter and complete freedom. His musical inspiration operates in a world uncluttered by conventional bar lines, conventional chord changes, and conventional ways of blowing or fingering a saxophone," and "we believe it is precisely because Mr. Coleman was not 'handicapped' by conventional music education that he has been able to make his unique contribution to contemporary music."[15]

This interpretation promoted Coleman by connecting him to what Daniel Belgrad calls "the culture of spontaneity."[16] Movements across the arts in the late 1950s linked spontaneity and authenticity. The belief that Coleman's music was freely improvised without standard technique allied it with the gestural painting of Abstract Expressionism. Before the term "free jazz" caught on, some critics called the music "action jazz," parallel to the "action painting" of Jackson Pollock et al., and a Pollock appeared on the cover of Coleman's 1961 *Free Jazz* LP.[17] This aesthetic similarly linked Coleman to the Beat movement in literature. For example, the first draft of Jack Kerouac's *On the Road*, published in 1957, was typed on a continuous scroll of paper to capture his spontaneous prose without interruption, and Allen Ginsberg used the Buddhist-derived phrase "first thought, best thought" to describe his process.

However, this mystique of spontaneity becomes less appealing when race is considered. Looking to racial Others for "intuitive" or "natural" alternatives to the neurosis of the modern West, whether Tibetan and Japanese Buddhists or African-American jazz musicians, risks exoticism, romanticization, and condescension. One notorious example is the 1957 essay "The White Negro," by Norman Mailer, who was a regular at the Five Spot. This text embraced African-Americans as icons of Beat or existential heroism through a collection of myths and stereotypes.[18] Schuller's comments linking Coleman's creativity to his lack of formal training illustrate jazz's complex position as a racialized intersection of art and entertainment. Would Schuller have written similarly about a white folk musician? Unfortunately, his selected writings only discuss jazz and classical music.[19]

There are also specifically musical factors that have produced and perpetuated mystery around Coleman's music of this period. First, most studies have analyzed Coleman's improvised solo lines in isolation, looking at their internal logic rather than that of the ensemble.[20] Second, many of his compositions have unusual sectional lengths or use different length forms for the melody and the solos.[21] For example, "Blues Connotation" (from Coleman's fifth album *This Is Our Music*) is two beats short of a twelve-bar blues the first time through the melody, then gets them back plus three extra bars the second time, but the solos don't follow this pattern.

On Coleman's Contemporary albums, without his regular band, the rhythm section usually rounded off his irregular compositions to standard twelve or thirty-two bar forms for improvising. On *The Shape of Jazz to Come* and *Change of the Century*, Charlie Haden and Billy Higgins sometimes play the odd forms, sometimes round them off, and sometimes do not play song form at all. After Ed Blackwell replaced Higgins on drums in 1961 for *This Is Our Music*, the band seldom played song forms, except for the blues.[22]

There are precedents in bebop for improvising on a simplified version of the form of the theme, such as Thelonious Monk's "I Mean You," which adds back a missing half bar, and Dizzy Gillespie's "A Night in Tunisia," which omits a sixteen-bar interlude, for using different chord changes for the solos than the theme, such as Monk's "Little Rootie Tootie" and Gillespie's "Salt Peanuts," which both use rhythm changes for the solos but not the theme, and even for using an unrelated and noncyclic tune to frame improvisations on a standard chord progression, as Charlie Parker did on "Ko-Ko."

In 1959, one could see performers representing almost the entire recorded history of jazz, from Louis Armstrong to Miles Davis, Coleman Hawkins to John Coltrane, Eubie Blake to Dave Brubeck, and they would all be improvising on song forms on every piece. Paul Bley, who led a quintet in Los Angeles in late 1958 with Coleman, Cherry, Haden, and Higgins, described the shock of learning Coleman's compositions: although he had played some completely free improvisations, he had not previously encountered music that approached form differently from piece to piece, what he called the "premise" of each song.[23]

Coleman's best-known composition, "Lonely Woman" from *The Shape of Jazz to Come*, is a dramatic example of such a premise. It features multiple innovations. First, the horns play the melody out of time, floating over a fast pulse in the drums. While rhythmic play, pushing and pulling the beat, is a major expressive element in jazz and part of what has been called "swing," "Lonely Woman" takes this to an extreme with the melody in a separate rhythmic universe from the drums. The theme follows an AABA form: in the A sections the horns play the melody while the bass strums a counterline in the middle register and drones the open D string, and in the B section the saxophone improvises against a rising chromatic line from the bass and trumpet with the drums landing strongly on their downbeats. Coleman is the only soloist and primarily uses the texture and tonality of the A section. After Coleman plays some figures closer to the blues than to the minor key of the theme, Cherry brings in the chromatic line from the B section, but the bass and drums do not join him. The solo can be heard as one AABA chorus with the length of those sections expanded, as a modal improvisation, or as a free exploration of ideas from the theme.[24]

In general, Coleman's premises fall into four categories. First, on some compositions the band plays a cyclic form, just like any other jazz band. To accompany the solos, the rhythm section loops a chord progression of a set length, usually based on the melody played at the beginning and end of the piece. This describes almost every piece on *Something Else!* and *Tomorrow Is the Question* and quite a few of those on *The Shape of Jazz to Come* and *Change of the Century*. "Turnaround," from *Tomorrow Is the Question*, follows a clear twelve-bar blues form throughout, and "Ramblin'" from *Change of the Century*, observes a novel form where swinging twelve-bar blues sections alternate with sixteen-bar ones based on Haden strumming the "Bo Diddley" beat.[25]

Second, starting on *The Shape of Jazz to Come*, they sometimes played what Ekkehard Jost calls "empty form": they kept the form of the composition for the solos but not its harmonic content, so a blues would still be twelve bars, probably in three phrases of four bars each, and maybe even with the second phrase a variation of the first, but it would not have any particular chord changes. On "Chronology," they apply this to rhythm changes.[26]

Explaining this requires a small amount of technical description. The chord progression in the A section of "I've Got Rhythm" is essentially a decoration of the tonic chord, while the B section starts with a chord that is outside of the key and works its way back moving steadily by fourths, landing on the dominant seventh chord, which is the strongest possible resolution to the tonic, returning to the A section.

On "Chronology," the band "plays rhythm changes without the changes," as Robert Hodson put it. They play four eight-bar sections, arranged AABA, with the A section closely orbiting the tonic and the B starting at a remove from it and returning in a longer arc, but they are not following any particular chord progression.[27] Charlie Haden explained:

> We weren't playing on changes like somebody would on "All the Things You Are," of course. But we were still respecting the songs how Ornette wrote them, with bridges and interludes.

Billy [Higgins] and I would still signify the new sections, even if we weren't playing the changes.[28]

Paul Bley described this type of improvising as, "You are going from point A to point B, and it's totally up to you what you want to do in that interval."[29] Similarly, Steve Lacy recalled Coleman explaining to him, "You just have a certain amount of space and you put whatever you want in it."[30] The structural markers still exist, but the musicians are free to pay them as much or as little attention as they wish. As Bley put it, "While Ornette was soloing on a 32-bar piece, suddenly he would play eight bars that had no relationship, or relatively little relationship to anything else in the piece. They were phrases he would play because they fit in eight bars."[31] It is important that these phrases fit the form, whether they match the harmony or not.

When musicians talk about this sort of playing being "outside," they often mean the player steps outside the harmony and comes back. This was not new with Coleman. Bebop musicians in particular had developed an assortment of harmonic devices that could be spontaneously superimposed on standard chord progressions. John Coltrane applied the harmonic cycles he developed for "Giant Steps" to various standard forms on several pieces from 1959 and 1960.[32] "Empty form" is different, because it is not systematic. As Lacy, Bley, and Haden said, although the group was aware of structural markers, their harmonic and formal role was optional. Unlike mainstream musicians using cycles and formulas to move inside and outside, the Coleman group did not reliably resolve, leaving those listening for functional harmony unsatisfied.

Third, the group sometimes treated form elastically. Ed Blackwell tells a story of Coleman criticizing him for playing a snare drum roll to mark the end of a chorus, Art Blakey–style, while Coleman was in the middle of a phrase.[33] Common practice is for the rhythm section to maintain the form and for soloists to play across its divisions if they wish, but Coleman wanted the form to stretch to accommodate his phrases. This is why many of the pieces on the first four albums have themes of irregular or inconsistent length, even when they are essentially twelve-bar blues or thirty-two-bar rhythm changes. Coleman preferred to expand and contract forms to fit his ideas rather than fitting his ideas into a form, and, once he was able to record with his choice of players, starting on *The Shape of Jazz to Come*, Coleman coached them to follow him.[34]

Fourth, the solo sections sometimes were truly free of form. Improvisations without a preset chord sequence, sectional plan, or number of bars were rarer on Coleman's first four albums than many assumed, but became more frequent on *This Is Our Music* and subsequent collections.[35]

Free

In his liner notes to *Change of the Century*, Coleman describes the piece "Free" as representing "free group improvising."[36] The composed melody is a rising and falling boogie-woogie figure played by the horns alone, with bass and drums contributing only isolated punctuation. It is eight bars long, stays close to a home key, and fits an AABA form, with a contrasting bass and drums interlude as the B section. This could set up an abstraction of rhythm changes, as on "Chronology," but "Free" is a different premise. Here, after the theme, Coleman's solo begins with Higgins playing fast swing and Haden briefly playing a three-beat cross-rhythm before joining him with walking bass. The solo ends with Higgins dropping out and Haden switching to irregular long tones behind Coleman, who hands off to Cherry, then Higgins reenters and the fast swing resumes. After Cherry's solo, a four-way improvised dialogue functions as a transition to the theme reprise.

Collective improvisation dominated early jazz but was largely replaced by individual solos with accompaniment beginning in the 1930s.[37] Some players associated with cool jazz had experimented with improvised counterpoint, including Jimmy Giuffre, Gerry Mulligan, Lee Konitz, Chet Baker, Jack Sheldon, Bob Brookmeyer, and Warne Marsh, but it was Coleman and Cherry's simultaneous playing that was greeted as a reintroduction of polyphony.[38] This reached its apex on the 1961 LP *Free Jazz*, where the four horns are not only featured in individual solos but also play at will throughout.[39]

Coleman's reference to "free group improvising" in the song "Free" may be about this collective passage, but it also describes what happens formally during his and Cherry's solos. Each improvises with no predetermined meter, harmony, or cyclic song form. The tonality of the theme exerts some influence, but it is optional. The bass mostly plays a quarter note walking line and the drums keep swinging time on the ride cymbal, producing the texture of bebop, but they are playing what became known as "time, no changes," creating harmonies, phrases, and sections in the moment.

The biggest challenge for the listener may be that Coleman and his band take multiple approaches to form, sometimes even within the same composition. They often do not play free from form but instead treat form freely. Strategies often differ between pieces and among musicians. If a song has implied chord changes, Don Cherry and Charlie Haden address them at least some of the time, but Coleman does not.[40] This is what Walter Norris, the pianist on *Something Else!*, meant when he said, "Ornette doesn't seem to know his own tunes": his improvising did not demonstrate a conventional understanding of harmony.[41]

Harmolodics

Coleman worked instead from a consistent alternative concept. He first used the word "harmolodics" to describe this in 1972, in the liner notes to the debut recording of his piece *Skies of America* for orchestra and improvisers, but its meaning has remained an enigma.[42] Harmolodics seems to be both what Stephen Rush calls "a metaphor for social and mystical principles seminal to the black American experience" and an alternative version of music theory.[43] Coleman's own texts are challenging, using musical terminology in uniquely personal and metaphorical ways, so authors have attempted to decode harmolodics from the recorded evidence, by observing Coleman's rehearsals, and by talking with his band members.[44]

Unison and transposition are frequent topics in harmolodics. "Unison" customarily means that musicians are playing together by playing identical pitches and rhythms: unity is established through conformity. However, for Coleman "unison" seems to mean that a group has achieved unity through diversity: everyone simultaneously playing an individual idea of the music in a distinct voice.

There is also a more technical musical side to this related to transposition. Most reeds and brass are transposing instruments, which means the pitches that come out of them are in a different key from those the performer reads. An alto saxophonist will read a C on their part but sound an E-flat, while a tenor saxophonist will see and finger that same note but produce a B-flat. This is tricky to get accustomed to, but enables musicians to read and finger uniformly across an entire instrument family: all the saxophones, all the clarinets, and so on.

The first musical scale taught is usually C major, the white keys of the piano, which run CDEFGABC, but when Coleman taught himself he assumed that musical letters would follow the order of the alphabet, beginning with A.[45] Coincidentally, the A on the alto saxophone sounds C, so when Coleman began playing with piano, guitar, and bass players, his A was their C. To confuse things further, the note read as an A in the treble clef is read as a C in the bass clef.

Coleman eventually became familiar with the adjustments made to achieve conventional unison but also continued to believe that each instrument had what he called its own unison, that the difference in pitch between an alto saxophone C and a trumpet C was part of the essential identity of those instruments that transposing them to achieve a conventional unison suppressed. *Skies of America* is the epitome of his alternative "harmolodic unison." Each member of the orchestra was given the identical notated melody. When the violins, flutes, and oboes saw a note in the third space of the staff, they read it as a treble clef C and sounded a C. The B-flat clarinets and trumpets read the same pitch and sounded a B-flat below that, which the French horns (which are in F) sounded an F below that. The violas read that same notation as a D in alto clef, and the cellos, bassoons, and trombones could read it as a B in tenor clef or join the basses and tuba reading it as an E in bass clef. The aggregate is the notes E B D F B-flat C, low to high.[46] *Skies of America* is almost entirely the orchestra playing melodies in this parallel block voicing while Coleman joins them in the alto saxophone key or improvises. However, this version of harmolodic unison does not explain much of what happened in his small groups, where most of the playing was improvisation by one horn with bass and drums and, while Coleman's electric band Prime Time often played in multiple keys at once, this was a compositional decision since his saxophone was the only transposing instrument.

Ekkehard Jost described Coleman's improvising logic as "motivic chain association," a musical parallel to the practice of free association in psychoanalysis and surrealism and stream of consciousness writing in modernist literature, which were Continental precursors to the American "culture of spontaneity."[47] In this account, Coleman puts one musical idea after another, like any improviser, but, like an analysand, he tells his story without intending or understanding its meaning. However, it is common for improvisers to approach a solo without planning, to assemble it as it happens after internalizing the form and suitable material. What actually makes Coleman different is his attitude to form, as discussed above, and his sense of what material is suitable. His associations are not unconscious but express a nonstandard conscious order.

Keyboardist Dave Bryant and guitarist Kenny Wessel played together in Prime Time for over a decade and remember Coleman constantly discussing systems of pitch organization. Both now give workshops and master classes on these techniques. Like most improvisers, Coleman practiced and studied his material intensely to be able to use it spontaneously in performance.

Bryant and Wessel observed that Coleman mainly used simple elements in his writing and improvising—major and minor scales and chords up to the seventh—but combined them in unconventional ways. In standard harmony, chords are built from alternate scale degrees. A chord consists of the first, third, and fifth notes of a scale: for example, C major is C, E, and G from CDEFGABC. These three are called a triad. The seventh can almost always be included, and bebop musicians also worked extensively with the ninth, eleventh, and thirteenth, the higher extensions. Rather than finding increasingly sophisticated approaches to standard progressions, as bebop and postbop players did, Coleman found new ways to sequence more basic material, making his music sound simultaneously strange and familiar.

In 1958, Coleman said, "I always write the melody line first because several different chords can fit the same melody line. In fact, I would prefer it if musicians would play my tunes with different changes as they take a new chorus so that there'd be all the more variety in the performance."[48] He was not referring to the systems of reharmonization and chord substitution that jazz musicians layer on functional harmony, but to what he later named harmolodics. In tonal harmony, chords move in patterns of tension and release, away from and back to a home key (resolution) or to a new key (modulation). Harmolodics adds other options. Coleman famously said he wanted to "play the music, not the background," which again implies that he improvised from the melody, not the harmony.[49] As guitarist James Blood Ulmer put it, for Coleman "the change comes after the phrase"; chords are derived from the melodic line, not from their functions in tonality.[50] Coleman's band members Don Cherry, Jimmy Garrison, and Al McDowell have attempted to explain harmolodics by describing how a note plays different roles in different chords: C is the root of C, the minor third of A, the major third of A-flat, the fifth of F, the minor seventh of D, and the major seventh of

D-flat.[51] Coleman's music unfolds based on these associations, not the syntax of resolution and modulation.

Wessel recalls Coleman teaching these relationships in sessions that initially seemed nonsensical. Coleman would ask, "What interval is A to B?" and the musicians would answer "a whole step" or "a major second," the traditionally correct answers. "No," he'd reply, "it's a fourth, because A is the fifth of D, B is the third of G, and D to G is a fourth. Now what's A to B?" "A fourth?" "No, it's a flatted fifth, because A is the major seventh of B-lat, B is the fifth of E, and B-flat to E is a flatted fifth," and so on. Having six possible roles for each pitch means any pair of pitches implies thirty-six possible chord movements, some of which, such as D to G, are common in functional harmony, and others, such as B-flat to E, are not.

Another approach to this concept was what Coleman called "ringing keys": learning what combinations of notes occurred in which keys. The notes C, F, and A, for example, appear in the C, F, and B-flat major scales, but the notes C, F, and B are only together in C major. Knowing which combinations of notes denote which keys facilitates moving among them. He similarly told the members of Prime Time that any two triads either had a common tone or had notes a half step apart, which meant one could move from any chord to any chord by using the common tone as a pivot or the half step as a leading tone. Coleman practiced these moves constantly, and they seem to be what he taught his band members and musicians who sought him out for lessons.[52] This is how Coleman spontaneously generated harmony from melody: his improvising was based on the possible harmonizations of the notes of a melody rather than the melodic implications of a set of chord changes.

Time, No Changes

The structural aspects of Coleman's method that were most easily identified and adopted by other musicians were empty form and "time, no changes." Paul Bley and Gary Peacock both applied techniques from free jazz in more mainstream settings. Bley's solo on "All the Things You Are" from Sonny Rollins's 1963 album *Sonny Meets Hawk* drew a Coleman-like line through the harmony and form clearly laid out by the bass and drums. It acknowledges the chord changes and bar lines just often enough to demonstrate that Bley is aware of them, but they did not determine the content of the solo. Bley described this as moving freely between the song and "a parallel universe."[53]

At the end of 1963, Peacock played on Bill Evans's album *Trio 64*. Peacock was also working with Bley and would shortly begin both performing regularly with Albert Ayler and substituting for Ron Carter in Miles Davis's quintet. Brought into Evans's trio by drummer Paul Motian, who also often played with Bley, Peacock seemed to pick up where Scott LaFaro left off, using the bass as a frontline partner to the piano at least as often as accompaniment, but sometimes clashing with Evans and record producer Creed Taylor over his "outside" choices. On "Santa Claus Is Coming to Town," he improvised by hearing the song's melody in his head while playing free, creating a solo that defies the bar lines and chord changes but lands exactly at the end of the form. Like Bley's "parallel universe" metaphor, Peacock described the form of a tune as the "ground." He doesn't consciously work with or against it, it is simply present, like the earth under his feet.[54]

This work influenced a subsequent generation of players, including some not frequently identified with free jazz. Multi-instrumentalist Ralph Towner, who recorded two duo albums with Peacock in the 1990s, told him at their first meeting that he was fascinated and challenged by the "Santa Claus" solo, and Pat Metheny, Bill Frisell, and Keith Jarrett have spoken about the inspiration of Bley's "All the Things You Are" solo.[55]

Composer and theorist George Russell was so impressed by Ornette Coleman's work that he rushed to include it in the 1959 second edition of his book *The Lydian Chromatic Concept of Tonal Organization for Improvisation*. Russell was part of a group around Miles Davis and Gil Evans whose discussions of aesthetics and music theory had helped inspire *Kind of Blue* and modal jazz.[56] His *Lydian Chromatic Concept* argued that the historic trajectory of jazz harmony was towards accepting the expressive potential of any note over any chord, so the sense of a "right-wrong" relationship was increasingly replaced by tonal gravity, how strongly the player was drawn to the harmonic center.[57] Russell uses the term "tonal gravity" much as Peacock does "ground": an improviser does not need to pay attention to tonal gravity any more than a person walking needs to mind physical gravity, but both are always felt. To Russell, Coleman seemed less bound by gravity's pull than any improviser before him, putting in question the prescriptive role of composition. He said of Coleman, "Since all tonalities are relative to each other, it doesn't really matter where he is in the tune."[58] This deconstructive approach leads to "time, no changes" playing. If "it doesn't really matter where he is in the tune," why maintain its form?

Several established musicians experimented with elements of Coleman's method. Jimmy Giuffre met and jammed with Coleman at the 1959 Lenox Jazz Workshop, where Coleman challenged him to play more spontaneously and emotionally, and Giuffre's group shared the bill when Coleman returned to the Five Spot in mid-1960.[59] While Giuffre's music had always included some experimental elements, his encounter with Coleman seemed to push him further in that direction, leading to the albums *Piece for Clarinet and String Orchestra/Mobiles* (1959), *Fusion* (1961), *Thesis* (1961), and *Free Fall* (1963), which all included substantial free improvisation.

Charles Mingus took the frontline of his band—trumpeter Ted Curson and woodwind player Eric Dolphy—to see Coleman at the Five Spot, then asked if they could play that way.[60] Their October 1960 recording *Charles Mingus Presents Charles Mingus* is the answer. It includes "All the Things You Could Be If Sigmund Freud's Wife Was Your Mother," which is a rhythmically elastic interpretation of "All the Things You Are" without the chord changes, "Folk Forms #1," which is a collective improvisation on the blues, and "What Love?," which is an out-of-time abstraction of the standard "What Is This Thing Called Love?" featuring a celebrated Dolphy/Mingus duet where they imitate a verbal argument. The only piece not formally responding to Coleman is Mingus's anti-racist anthem "Original Faubus Fables," but the sound of the pianoless quartet itself refers to Coleman's, with Dolphy usually on alto saxophone and Curson using a pocket trumpet like Don Cherry's.

John Coltrane also attended many of Coleman's Five Spot shows, befriended him, and even paid him for several lessons in his concept. In the summer of 1960 Coltrane recorded an album of Coleman's music with Coleman's band—Don Cherry, Charlie Haden, and Ed Blackwell—explaining that he was seeking an alternative to the harmonically dense approach of "Giant Steps."[61]

Sonny Rollins hired Cherry and Billy Higgins for a weekend at the Village Gate in the summer of 1962, with Bob Cranshaw on bass, documented on the 1962 LP *Our Man in Jazz* and a more complete recent semi-bootleg, followed by a winter European tour with Henry Grimes on bass. This quartet played Rollins's usual repertoire of original compositions and jazz standards with Coleman-inspired elasticity and polyphony, as well as some pieces that seem to have been completely improvised.

Rollins followed this project with *Sonny Meets Hawk* in 1963, with Paul Bley on piano. His next two albums, *Now's the Time* and *The Standard Sonny Rollins*, consisted of more orderly and concise performances, with Herbie Hancock replacing Bley.

Hancock was concurrently recording for Blue Note as a leader and working as a member of Miles Davis's group, which has become known as the Second Great Quintet. While Davis was an outspoken critic of free jazz players, including Coleman, Don Cherry, Cecil Taylor, Archie Shepp, and Eric Dolphy, the members of his rhythm section—Hancock, Ron Carter, and Tony Williams—had all worked with Dolphy. Hancock, Williams, and saxophonist Wayne Shorter notably used and developed elements of free jazz in their work away from Davis, including Williams's albums *Spring* and *Life Time*, Shorter's *The All-Seeing Eye*, "Survival of the Fittest" from Hancock's *Maiden Voyage*, and "The Egg" from his *Empyrean Isles*, as well as Williams's appearances on Dolphy's *Out to Lunch*, Grachan Moncur III's *Some Other Stuff* (along with Shorter and Hancock), Jackie McLean's *Vertigo*, Sam Rivers's *Fuchsia Swing Song* (with Carter), and Andrew Hill's *Point of Departure*.[62]

These elements also appeared when they played with Davis, despite his public distance from the new music. When Buster Williams substituted for Ron Carter with Davis, he "learned how to keep a structure in mind and play changes so loosely that you can play for some time without people knowing whether the structure is played or not, but then hit on certain points to indicate that you have been playing the structure all the time," which sounds quite similar to Haden, Peacock, and Bley's descriptions of their approaches to song form.[63] The quintet applied this technique, "time, no changes," metric modulation, and other "outside" approaches to Davis's standard repertoire, deliberately contradicting conventions and expectations, which Tony Williams called "playing anti-music," on *Live at the Plugged Nickel*, recorded in December 1965.[64]

On the 1967 LP *Miles Smiles*, Hancock does not play chords behind Davis and Shorter's solos and plays only horn-like single lines in his own, simulating the pianoless texture and harmonic freedom of Coleman's groups.[65] "Orbits" and "Dolores," from *Miles Smiles*, and "Pinocchio," "Hand Jive," and "Madness" from 1968's *Nefertiti* all used the "time, no changes" approach for some or all of the solos, and this was increasingly common live, becoming the default approach on Davis's 1967 European tour.[66] When Chick Corea, Dave Holland, and Jack DeJohnette replaced Hancock, Carter, and Williams during 1968 and 1969, free playing continued to dominate Davis's live sets, although the band also adopted electric piano and bass guitar and began interpreting the groove-based material recorded in 1969 for *In a Silent Way* and *Bitches Brew*. Contemporary reception of this music focused on these "jazz-rock fusion" aspects rather than the free jazz ones.[67]

Similarly, Keith Jarrett, Corea's successor in Davis's keyboard chair, has always been seen as part of the jazz mainstream rather than the avant-garde, even dipping into crossover as a member of the rock-friendly Charles Lloyd Quartet in the mid-1960s and with his solo piano recordings of the 1970s. However, when he began working as a leader after leaving Lloyd, his trio included Charlie Haden and Paul Motian. This became a quartet in 1971 with the addition of saxophonist Dewey Redman, previously part of Ornette Coleman's group. Jarrett did not play like a "free jazz pianist," but he surrounded himself with free jazz players and created an eclectic music that encompassed all their interests, from gospel vamps to "time, no changes" to exotica.[68]

Pat Metheny notably collaborated with Haden, Redman, Billy Higgins, and Coleman himself on the albums *Rejoicing*, *Beyond the Missouri Sky*, *80/81*, and *Song X*, recorded Coleman's "Round Trip" and "Broadway Blues" on his debut *Bright Size Life* and "Law Years" on *Question and Answer*, and used the "time, no changes" approach in his own music, particularly the title track of *Offramp*.[69]

"Time, no changes" became a regular improvisational form for the generations of free jazz players who followed Coleman. Numerous examples occur in the music of the Archie Shepp/Bill Dixon Quartet ("Quartet"), the New York Contemporary Five ("Consequences," "Rufus"), Marion Brown ("27 Cooper Square"), John Carter ("In the Vineyard," "Sticks and Stones"), and many others. In the 1970s, it appeared often in the work of Sam Rivers (*Trio Live*, "Rapture," "Expectation"), Dave Holland ("Four Winds," "See-Saw"), Fred Anderson ("Saxoon"), Jimmy Lyons *(Jump Up)*, and Anthony Braxton (Compositions 6I, 23B, 23D, 23J, 40B, and 40K), among many others.

The "Young Lions" movement of the 1980s was promoted as a return to the mainstream jazz tradition, reacting against free jazz, fusion, and crossover/smooth/pop jazz. However, Wynton Marsalis's debut album featured the Hancock/Carter/Williams rhythm section from Miles Davis's Second Great Quintet, and both he and his brother Branford often employed "time, no changes," which they called "burnout," exemplified by "No Backstage Pass" from Branford's *Scenes in the City* and "LonJellis" from his *Random Abstract*. Both Marsalis brothers later paid direct homage to Coleman: Branford by recording his piece "Giggin'" on his *Footsteps of Our Fathers* album and Wynton by performing evenings of his music with the Jazz at Lincoln Center Orchestra.

Their embrace of Coleman is based on their understanding of his relationship to the jazz tradition. Branford writes about listening to *The Shape of Jazz to Come*:

> I had often heard Ornette's music described as "out," which probably contributed to my confusion when hearing it. After three months of continuous listening, I realized that some of the forms of the songs were quite traditional, and that Mr. Coleman had figured out a way to expand the edges of traditional form, a complete contradiction of the modern definition of innovation. His ability to play traditional song forms while avoiding the trap of playing in four- and eight-bar phrases was much of the basis for my future development.[70]

The implicit definition of "innovation" as negation here is a straw man, assuming that only musicians who completely defy convention are seen as innovative, and the entire argument rests on Coleman's connection to standard forms, assuming that music outside of the common practice of jazz is not jazz.[71] Compare this to contemporary art, which has no common practice and neither a center nor limits, where the category of sculpture easily includes Damien Hirst's taxidermy shark, Richard Serra's steel walls, and Tracy Emin's soiled mattress.

Free jazz musicians are sometimes accused of playing the way they do because they can't play "normally," that they are "too lazy" to learn how to properly navigate chord changes, and so on.[72] While some free jazz players such as Arthur Blythe and Anthony Braxton have recorded standards albums to demonstrate their connection to "the tradition," in the mid-1960s Coleman made two major moves in the opposite direction, leaning into questions of how work can have meaning and value if it defies common practice.

Coleman first recorded playing trumpet and violin on "Snowflakes and Sunshine" from his 1965 album *At the Golden Circle*, volume 2. He was self-taught on both instruments and his approach, especially on violin, was intuitive and gestural, ignoring standard technique and vocabulary. On his next LP, *The Empty Foxhole*, he used his ten-year-old son Denardo on drums. Some musicians, including trumpet players Miles Davis, Freddie Hubbard, and Lee Morgan, found these choices an insult, a gesture of disrespect to the work they had put into mastering their instruments.[73] Drummer Shelly Manne, who had played on Coleman's *Tomorrow Is the Question*, called *The Empty Foxhole* "unadulterated shit" in *Downbeat* magazine.[74]

Coleman's decisions to pick up the trumpet and violin and to perform with his child came from a deep and literally naive faith in spontaneity, in authentic expression unfiltered by training, assumptions, memory, expectation, pretense, ambition, vanity, or any other form of self-consciousness.[75] By breaking with the common practice of jazz, he suspended its technical and aesthetic assumptions, opening a space where artists could invent and explore their own concepts of order and value. While his album title *The Shape of Jazz to Come* declared that it contained the music of the future, it was followed shortly by *This Is Our Music*, which carries an implied challenge and invitation to others' creativity: "This is our music, what's yours?"

2

Spirituality

John Coltrane had dental surgery in May 1959, right after the sessions that produced "Giant Steps" and "Countdown," his masterpieces of harmonic density. He continued playing live with Miles Davis, and occasionally as a leader, but took a break from recording.[1] Davis maintained a busy touring schedule through 1960, playing standard repertoire and music from *Kind of Blue*. When Coltrane returned to his own music that October, he had assembled what would become known as his classic quartet, with McCoy Tyner on piano, Elvin Jones on drums, and Steve Davis, Reggie Workman, and Jimmy Garrison passing through the bass chair. The music they made in the first half of the 1960s combined modal playing with inspiration from other cultures, spirituality, and politics to popularize new structures and subject matter in jazz.

Their interpretation of "My Favorite Things" from the then-current Broadway musical *The Sound of Music* was an unexpected hit and remained in Coltrane's repertoire for the rest of his career. It revived interest in the soprano saxophone and expanded the concept of "modal jazz" from *Kind of Blue*.[2] Richard Rogers's original composition was a simple waltz appropriate to the Austrian setting of the show, but Coltrane's arrangement draws from more international sources. Jones plays an African-derived pattern alternating two groups of three beats and three groups of two rather than the straight three of a European waltz beat, and the improvisations are based on two tonal areas of the song: E minor and E major, each played for as long as the soloist wants rather than following the form or chord changes. Changing modes over a drone is common in Indian music, which Coltrane began to investigate during this period, and Indian music also provided a model for maintaining interest over static harmony through intense interaction between soloist and percussion.[3] There is little improvisation by the piano and bass during the long saxophone solo; they provide steady support for the flowing dialogue between Coltrane and Jones.

Miles Davis drew subtly from sources outside of jazz and popular song for *Kind of Blue*, naming one piece "Flamenco Sketches" and basing the piano introduction to "All Blues" on the kalimba playing he heard accompanying a performance by *Les Ballet Africains* from Guinea.[4] His next album, *Sketches of Spain*, featured Spanish-inspired modal playing backed by a large ensemble. In May 1961, Coltrane led two sessions that continued exploring international sources for modal improvisation. *Olé* added trumpeter Freddie Hubbard, saxophonist/flutist/bass clarinetist Eric Dolphy, and second bassist Art Davis to the quartet. Its title track uses a Spanish folk song to frame improvising on a flamenco-inspired vamp, while "Dahomey Dance" uses the two basses to emulate a recording of African log drums.[5] *Africa/Brass* also augmented the quartet with a second bassist, plus a brass section playing Dolphy's arrangements of Tyner's piano voicings. Coltrane's composition "Africa" filled the first side of the LP, with a long tenor solo over one chord, French horn glissandi evoking animal cries, and a drum feature, while the second side included a blues and an arrangement of the English folk song "Greensleeves" using a similar 6/8 groove and modal alternation to "My Favorite Things."

At the start of November 1961, Impulse recorded Coltrane's quartet, joined by Dolphy and with Workman and Garrison sharing the bass chair, live at the Village Vanguard. This music was released in part on 1962's *"Live" at the Village Vanguard* and 1963's *Impressions*, then in a series of increasingly complete posthumous collections. The title track of *Impressions* is a melody Coltrane put over the form of "So What," from *Kind of Blue*, linking back to that landmark of modal jazz.[6] The other long piece on the album, "India," is based on a piece from a Folkways album of Vedic chant.[7] Like "Africa," it features long solos over unchanging harmony. Coltrane's interest in music beyond jazz and European and American classical and popular musics was facilitated by the increasing availability of field recordings on Folkways and other specialized labels during the 1950s and by more popular releases by Ravi Shankar, Babatunde Olatunji, and others.

"India" includes Ahmed Abdul-Malik, a bassist who had worked with Coltrane in Thelonious Monk's quartet, playing the tamboura, which traditionally provides the drone characteristic of Indian classical music. Malik's own work as a leader combined modal jazz with Arabic music and featured him playing melodies on the oud before picking up the bass to accompany his band members.[8]

Besides including the tamboura, Coltrane tried unsuccessfully to get Indian virtuosi Ravi Shankar and Alla Rakha to play sitar and tabla with his band at the Vanguard. Elvin Jones met Rakha in 1961 and may have been inspired by him to use a *tihai*, a rhythmic fill repeated three times and aligned so that the third repetition will end on the downbeat of the next section, on "India" and "Chasin' the Trane" from the Vanguard sessions.[9]

"India" is unusual among Coltrane's 1961 "world music" pieces in emulating its inspiration this literally or in this much detail. However, the solos on "India" do not follow a raga any more than those on "Olé" respect the conventions of flamenco.[10] The improvisers approach the drone as fluidly and obliquely as they would a standard tune or the blues. Listening closely to the solos on *Kind of Blue* and Coltrane's 1961 recordings reveals that modal jazz was a compositional approach more than an improvisational one. The key characteristics of Davis and Coltrane's modal material are the slow rate of harmonic change: every eight or sixteen bars in "So What" and "Impressions," on cue in "My Favorite Things" and "Flamenco Sketches," or never in "Africa" and "India," and the frequent use of chords built on fourths or superimposed on bass notes outside of the chord.[11] While "time, no changes" and modal playing freed improvisers from navigating chord changes and song forms, they also removed the built-in narratives of tension and resolution those elements offered, requiring the players to create their own.

Coltrane's interest in Africa and India was not only a search for new sounds. Deconstructing the form and harmony of "My Favorite Things" to a cued alternation between major and minor and playing "Africa" and "India" on a single chord each reduced the American popular and European classical elements in the music. For Coltrane, modal and pentatonic sounds represented a "universal aspect of music" transcending and uniting the African, Indian, English, and Spanish sources he tapped in 1961.[12] He was reading the Bhaghavad Gita and Paramahansa Yogananda's *Autobiography of a Yogi* at the same time that he was getting to know Indian music through Ravi Shankar.[13]

These spiritual interests paralleled political events. African decolonization unfolded quickly, with over a dozen nations throwing off European rule in 1960 alone. While Coltrane never dedicated a piece to African liberation like Lee Morgan's "Mr. Kenyatta" or Randy Weston's *Uhuru Afrika*, he was clearly among those looking outside the US for creative, spiritual, and political inspiration.

At the same time, he was not ignoring his own religious background, his folk heritage, or American politics. "Spiritual," from the Vanguard sessions, introduced a key element of Coltrane's 1960s music that trumpet player Bobby Bradford has dubbed "the incantatory intro."[14] "Spiritual" begins with Coltrane playing a minor pentatonic theme out of time over a rolling pedal tone and Jones playing the drums with mallets, then moves into a two-chord vamp in the band's familiar Africanized waltz groove for the solos. The theme is an alternate folk melody to "Nobody Knows De Trouble I See," from James Weldon Johnson's *The Book of Negro Spirituals*, which Coltrane is known to have owned.[15]

Establishing modal and thematic material in an out-of-time prelude is common in Indian music, where it's called an *alap*, and Arabic music, where it is called a *taqsim*, as well as in Japanese *gagaku*.[16] However, it also has the incantatory element Bradford named. More than musical resources are being invoked. Drummer Garth Powell refers to this free jazz form of a meditative introduction over a drone leading into more energized solos as "summoning the spirits, then becoming possessed by them."[17] These incantations are also closely tied to language, resembling recitative passages from opera or cantillation of passages from the Torah or Koran: semi-improvised free-time modal expositions of text.

Attorney General Robert Kennedy had asked the Interstate Commerce Commission to officially desegregate interstate bus travel in May 1961, responding to the Freedom Rides. Their order took effect November 1, which was the first night of John Coltrane's engagement at the Vanguard and the night "Spiritual" was recorded.[18] Coltrane never mentioned this; it may have been a coincidence. However, his "Alabama," recorded two and a half years later, was a major statement on the civil rights movement. On September 15, 1963, white supremacists bombed a church in Birmingham, killing four children, reacting against the city's move to desegregate the public schools after months of protest. Recorded November 18, "Alabama" follows a similar outline to "Spiritual," with an incantation framing a solo in time over one chord but, instead of being based on a precomposed theme, the introduction embraces the recitative or cantorial model; it's Coltrane's spontaneous rendition of a Martin Luther King, Jr., speech, in the same C minor tonality as "Spiritual" and concluding with a similar descending unison gesture.[19] Although it was a studio recording, "Alabama" appeared on *Live at Birdland* in January 1964, suggesting Coltrane wanted to release it as soon as possible.

Besides external references to diverse musical traditions, belief systems, texts, and world events, Coltrane created what Scott Saul calls a "sense of spiritual drama" through musical devices including pedal points, sustained dissonances, repetitions, and long solos. The prolonged exploration of a small amount of material over a static tonality models focused searching while sustained polyrhythms and a lack of harmonic change create a trance-like suspension of time passing, and there is heavy use of call and response between the soloist and ensemble and within the soloist's own line, as in many religious observances.[20]

A Love Supreme

Coltrane's suite *A Love Supreme*, recorded by his quartet in December 1964, was an explicitly devotional work. It presented free jazz improvisation as a religious practice: not a representation of the experience, but the thing itself.[21] It was also remarkably successful, nominated for two Grammys, winning *Downbeat*'s Album of the Year, and selling over half a million copies by 1970.[22]

These themes and materials were not unique to Coltrane. Spirituals had been presented in jazz contexts at least since the 1939 "From Spirituals to Swing" concerts, and hard bop musicians wrote gospel pastiches such as Horace Silver's "The Preacher" and Charles Mingus's "Better Git It in Your Soul."[23] Duke Ellington's 1958 version of his *Black, Brown, and Beige* suite featured Mahalia Jackson singing his spiritual-inspired "Come Sunday" as part of a portrait of African-American culture, while Mary Lou Williams's 1962 mass *Black Christ of the Andes* and Ellington's sacred concerts, which began in 1965, were intended for performance in churches.[24]

Each movement of *A Love Supreme* employed a different structure common in the quartet's repertoire. The first is open playing over a bass vamp, the second is a song form, the third is a blues, and the fourth is a recitative. All four center on the pitches of an F minor pentatonic scale (F, A-flat, B-flat, C, and E-flat). While the piece's climax occurs during Coltrane's solo in the third movement, the first and last sections make this piece unique through their relationships to its theme, its text, and Coltrane's voice, as Lewis Porter has described in his definitive exegesis.[25]

At the end of his saxophone solo in section one, Coltrane plays the interval pattern of the bass line: root, up to the minor third, back down to the root, and up to the fourth, in rhythmic unison with the bass but moving it to almost every key. When he lands back in F with the bass, instead of playing the saxophone Coltrane sings the words "a love supreme" to the riff. Porter explains that Coltrane has performed "a reverse development," revealing the meaning of this melodic motif and the piece at the end of his solo. Rather than being confronted with an initial declaration of faith, the listener has gone on a search with Coltrane and arrived with him at his conclusion "that God is everywhere—in every register, in every key."[26]

This technique of approaching musical material as interval sets (root, minor 3, fourth) rather than pitches (F, A-flat, B-flat) became increasingly central to Coltrane's work, with these sets often replacing modes and tonal centers as the primary structural elements.[27] If jazz is freed from vertical harmony and cyclic form, exploring related melodic shapes using different pitches is another way to create coherence.

The last movement of *A Love Supreme* is the ultimate version of the incantatory intros from "Spiritual" and "Alabama," even unfolding over the same C pedal tone. Here, however, it is the concluding statement rather than a prelude. Coltrane published an original poem of praise and thanks to God as the liner notes to *A Love Supreme*, and for the album's conclusion he plays this poem on the saxophone, as he had Dr. King's speech for "Alabama."[28] This performance is not a representation of religious observance; it is literally prayer.

When Coltrane's quartet toured the West Coast in late 1965, they made several recordings with added guests, including nightclub sets mixing standards and free improvisations (*Live in Seattle*), a rare live performance of *A Love Supreme*, and ritualistic pieces inspired by texts (*Om* and "Kulu Se Mama"). *Om*, recorded October 1 in Seattle, is a half-hour excerpt from a six-hour session by the quartet with Pharoah Sanders (tenor saxophone), Joe Brazil (flute), and Donald Rafael Garrett (clarinet and bass).[29] The musicians also play additional percussion that Garrett brought to the session. After a short atmospheric passage led by kalimba and small bells, the musicians recite lines from the Bhaghavad Gita, there is a dense collective improvisation, and Elvin Jones kicks the rhythm section into formation to accompany solos by Coltrane, Sanders, and Tyner.[30] After a bass duet, all the players reenter, build layers of texture and conversation, and finally cut back to the original percussion and recitation.

Reception of *Om* has been affected by the multiple anonymous accounts that the band took LSD for this session.[31] These are cited both by some admirers, who hear the record as a genuine document of a psychedelic experience, and some detractors, who dismiss it as a spaced-out mess. Whatever the biographical truth, discussions of Coltrane, psychedelics, and mysticism illustrate that spiritual jazz developed as part of the 1960s counterculture. *A Love Supreme* is a linked set of compositions embodying ideas about faith as an offering to God, but *Om* attempts to push the music even farther, to use free group improvisation as a ritual to attain higher consciousness, with or without chemical help.

Universal Consciousness

Pharoah Sanders became a regular member of Coltrane's group following the fall 1965 West Coast tour, and Rashied Ali joined as a second drummer. After this sextet recorded *Meditations* in late November, McCoy Tyner and Elvin Jones quit, unhappy with the changing musical direction, especially the combined volume and conflicting approaches of the two drummers.[32] John Coltrane's wife, Alice, who had a notable career playing bebop and mainstream jazz with Terry Gibbs and others before their marriage, took over on piano, and the group continued as a quintet.

After John Coltrane's death in July 1967, Alice Coltrane and Pharoah Sanders further developed the international and devotional aspects of his music, defining the "spiritual jazz" idiom. Following the example of *A Love Supreme*, all of Alice Coltrane's music either represented her spiritual experiences or was an offering to God and employed a similar musical palette: pentatonic scales and fourths harmonies, vamps, out-of-time chant or prayer-like melodies, cued harmonic changes, dynamic ensemble interaction, and the blues.[33] Like John Coltrane, she believed modal music, especially pentatonic scales, expressed a "universal aspect of music" that transcended cultural difference and could articulate the divine.[34] The albums she made for Impulse between 1967 and 1973 increasingly revived the intercultural aspects of John Coltrane's early 1960s work and presented what she called "a totality concept," representing the universality of God through similarly universal music.[35]

The title track of her 1971 LP *Journey in Satchidananda*, named for her religious teacher Swami Satchidananda Saraswati, exemplifies this concept. It has no theme, consisting entirely of solos by her on harp and

Pharoah Sanders on soprano saxophone over a two-chord vamp in a rolling triple-meter groove, like the solo section of "Spiritual" and other pieces by John Coltrane's classic quartet. The bass line stays essentially the same throughout the piece and functions as the melodic hook. There is no piano on "Journey in Satchidananda"; Alice Coltrane only plays harp. Instead, the rhythm section is filled out by a tamboura drone, adding an Indian element to the bass and drum groove, advancing the "totality concept."

In John Coltrane's band, Sanders was often in the unenviable position of soloing on tenor saxophone after a marathon solo on the same instrument by the bandleader. In that situation he often concentrated on extended techniques, producing screams, honks, and growls. Sanders only plays soprano saxophone on *Journey in Satchidananda*, and on the title track he plays with an undistorted tone. He and Alice Coltrane stay almost completely within the mode on their solos, in contrast to John Coltrane and Eric Dolphy's more oblique harmonic approaches on "India" and John Coltrane's other 1961 modal pieces. Despite the title "Journey in Satchidananda," the piece is largely static. It maintains one tonality, groove, dynamic level, and mood. Unlike *A Love Supreme* and *Om*, which represent or perform a search for higher consciousness, it expresses Alice Coltrane's security that she has found her teacher. She spoke of improvisation as a voyage, but used serene and contemplative imagery:

> Avant-garde music to me is like journeying across the country until you come to a beautiful park. You say, "We'll stop here for just a moment." After a while you decide to go onward because you know of a nice area ahead, but before you leave, you see a lake that you didn't notice before, and you decide to stay and experience that for a while. Sometimes your moment is there like an eternity. That type of thing is quite prevalent in my music.[36]

The Nubians of Plutonia

In 1956, five years before John Coltrane, Sun Ra and his Arkestra also recorded a piece entitled "India." Atmospheric, percussion-heavy, and harmonically static, its tom-tom beats and pentatonic solos evoke clichés used to signify East Asian and Native American music, not India. It most closely resembles the "exotica" of Les Baxter and Martin Denny, white composers who led studio orchestras in instrumental fantasies of mysterious lands. Ra's music of the late 1950s connected the romantic and exotic sides of jazz composers like Ellington and Henderson with those of European composers like Scriabin and Debussy and of "mood music" bandleaders like Baxter and Denny. His *The Nubians of Plutonia*, recorded in the late 1950s, included pieces entitled "Africa," "Nubia," "Watusa," and "Aethiopia," as well as "Plutonian Nights," all using jazz, Latin, Caribbean, and mood music elements.[37] Ra read biblical and colonial geographies and tropes against the grain and merged them with science fiction to create alternative origin stories for African-Americans.[38]

Alice Coltrane created "Journey in Satchidananda" anticipating her trip to India.[39] Like Sun Ra and John Coltrane's Indias, it represents escape, inspiration, and enlightenment through a place she hasn't been. Exoticism runs through much spiritual jazz, but as a liberatory construct connoting pan-African and third world solidarity and religious knowledge transcending human difference rather than the sonic tourism of Baxter and Denny.

Nigerian percussionist Babatunde Olatunji was a key link between jazz, exotica, and "world music." While attending college in the US, he was struck by Americans' ignorance of Africa and formed a drumming and dance group to remedy this, although he was not from a traditional drumming lineage. In the late 1950s, Olatunji dropped out of graduate school to pursue music full time and soon signed to Columbia Records.[40] His debut, *Drums of Passion*, was released in April 1960, the same month as Miles Davis's *Sketches of Spain*, and was a massive hit.[41] While the label initially balked at the word "passion" in the title and Olatunji insisted it referred only to the sincerity of the performance, the erotic and exotic are often linked.[42]

Drums of Passion was a hybrid of Nigerian and Ghanian elements. It presented concise and clearly structured songs representing Africa as simultaneously exotic and universal, mysterious and accessible, and coincided with the height of African decolonization.[43] Olatunji fronted a group of African-American and Afro-Caribbean drummers who used exotic stage names. Roger "Montego Joe" Sanders was a first-generation Jamaican immigrant, Thomas "Taiwo" DuVall's grandparents were Jamaican, and James Hawthorne "Chief" Bey was African-American.[44] After its release, Olatunji's own playing added an African touch to mainstream jazz records by Herbie Mann, Kai Winding, and Cannonball Adderley, Randy Weston's celebration of African decolonization *Uhuru Afrika*, and, with DuVall, the second side of Max Roach's *We Insist! Max Roach's Freedom Now Suite*, which juxtaposed African and African-American liberation struggles.[45]

Olatunji and his band members also collaborated with free jazz musicians. Yusef Lateef and John Coltrane helped support Olatunji's Center for African Culture in Harlem, their bands and his often shared bills, Coltrane named his composition "Tunji" for Olatunji, and Coltrane's last known recording comes from a performance at the center.[46] Sun Ra also knew Olatunji; his *Atlantis* LP was recorded live at the center and his saxophonists Pat Patrick and Marshall Allen played on Olatunji's 1965 album *Drums! Drums! Drums!*[47] Montego Joe led a Latin band in the early 1960s that included Chick Corea, Eddie Gomez, and Milford Graves, then had a long and varied career as a session musician, while Chief Bey played on Pharoah Sanders's early 1970s *Thembi* and *Izipho Zam (My Gifts)* albums. This constellation of relationships illustrates some of the complexity of diasporic, hybrid, and created identities in these musical communities.

New Africa

At the end of July 1969, Archie Shepp's band appeared at the First Annual Pan-African Festival in Algiers, joined by poets Ted Joans and Don L. Lee and a group of Tuareg musicians playing reeds and percussion. As recorded on *Live at the Pan-African Festival*, Shepp on tenor saxophone, Clifford Thornton on cornet, and Grachan Moncur III on trombone interacted with the Tuareg ensemble and stepped out for solos, but the contributions of Dave Burrell on piano, Alan Silva on bass, and Sunny Murray on drums were mostly inaudible.

The Pan-African Festival not only brought Shepp and his band to Africa for the first time and put them on stage with indigenous musicians but brought them to a nation whose recent struggle for independence from French colonialism had produced Franz Fanon's book *The Wretched of the Earth* and the film *The Battle of Algiers*, important texts for radicals in the United States. Algiers also was a nexus between African-American and third world revolutionaries. Other festival performers included Nina Simone and Miriam Makeba, who had left South Africa for the US only to marry Black Power activist Stokley Carmichael (Kwame Ture) and join him in political exile. Black Panther Eldridge Cleaver had moved to Algiers in June 1969, after jumping bail on charges related to a shootout with Oakland police, and was a large presence at the festival. The American artists and activists found themselves in the middle of a debate among African revolutionaries about the ongoing relevance of the Negritude movement, parallel to that between Marxists and cultural nationalists in the African-American vanguard.[48] Joans and Lee's declarations during Shepp's set that "We are Black, and we have come back," "Jazz is a Black power," "Jazz is an African power," and "Jazz is African music," were an unrefined intervention in this debate, audibly appreciated by the audience.[49]

Just over a week later in Paris, Shepp and his band joined in several days of recording sessions for the BYG Actuel label that mixed touring and expatriate American musicians with a handful of Europeans. These included several pieces inspired by their Algerian experience. Burrell said, "We were so high off of the experience of playing in Algeria that Paris seemed like dessert after the main course. It was like going to a big party every morning. Who are you going to record with today?"[50]

The title track of Moncur's *New Africa*, recorded August 11 with Burrell, Silva, Cecil Taylor's drummer Andrew Cyrille, and Roscoe Mitchell of the Art Ensemble of Chicago on alto saxophone and piccolo, uses pentatonic melodies over vamps and fourths chords to frame solos over 4/4 swing and static modal harmony. Although Moncur had recorded this piece with Shepp in New York in February, performing in Africa may have inspired him to revisit it. The next day, Mitchell, Burrell, Thornton, and Murray were part of the eleven-piece group that recorded Shepp's "Yasmina, a Black Woman." Based on a two-chord piano vamp reinforced by the horns, propelled by two basses, and centering on a long tenor solo by the leader, it also evokes a hybrid African identity by featuring the log drum, played in several West and Central African cultures, the West African balafon, and shouts of *uhuru*, Swahili for "freedom." Almost half of Sunny Murray's "Suns of Africa Pt. 1," recorded by a similar large group on the 15th, is an incantatory rubato dialogue between Mitchell and Kenneth Terroade on flutes, accompanied by small bells and gongs, before Burrell and vocalist Jeanne Lee introduce a chant-like pentatonic vamp. During a balafon solo, horns, basses, and drum set join the vamp, which then accompanies collective improvising by Mitchell, Shepp, and Terroade on saxophones, joined after a minute or two by the brass section: Moncur, Thornton, and Lester Bowie of the Art Ensemble. "Touareg," an intense free improvisation recorded on August 16 by Shepp, Art

Ensemble bassist Malachi Favors, and expatriate bebop drummer Philly Joe Jones, captures the energy of the festival performance, but uses no North African elements.

"New Africa," "Yasmina, a Black Woman," and "Suns of Africa" are all in the "spiritual jazz" idiom John Coltrane introduced between 1960 and 1965, demonstrating how deeply it had become identified with Black political and racial consciousness. Shepp and his band members reflected on their experience of the actual Africa using materials from the constructed Africas of John Coltrane, Olatunji, and others.

Karma

While Shepp's sextet was in Paris, Pharoah Sanders's album *Karma* debuted at number five on the *Billboard* jazz chart. It continued to chart for three months.[51] This is remarkable for any free jazz record, especially one dominated by a single thirty-two-minute piece: "The Creator Has a Master Plan." Despite its length, this track may be the closest free jazz got to a hit single. Sanders had developed a more accessible version of John Coltrane's spiritual jazz style which could cross over to rock and R and B audiences.

On one hand, the turn to spirituality in jazz was at odds with established contexts for jazz performance and the conception of jazz as light entertainment. As musicians came to see themselves as artists rather than entertainers, they objected to playing in clubs where selling drinks took priority over their music. Charles Mingus was particularly notorious for confronting intrusive servers and noisy or inattentive audiences and gamely recreated one of these harangues on the album *Charles Mingus Presents Charles Mingus*. John Coltrane, from all accounts a much gentler man than Mingus, echoed some of his concerns: "There are a lot of times it doesn't make sense, man, to have somebody drop a glass, or somebody ask for some money right in the middle of Jimmy Garrison's solo. I think the music is rising into something else, and so we'll have to find this kind of place to be played in."[52]

While the dialectic between Saturday night and Sunday morning has been crucial to much African-American music, explicitly devotional music was a particularly bad fit with nightclubs. Pharoah Sanders was among the musicians who, inspired by John Coltrane's lifestyle, became vegetarians, started doing yoga, and preferred to not have their music used to promote drinking or other vices.⁵³ Part of the reason John Coltrane, Yusef Lateef, and Olatunji started the Center for African Culture was to have a wholesome performance space focused on listening.⁵⁴ In some cases, spiritual jazz moved completely to Sunday morning, becoming liturgical music. Alice Coltrane left public life in 1975 to open the Vedantic Center.⁵⁵ She made exclusively sacred music, performed by her disciples and distributed on cassette within her religious community, until returning to jazz for a final album in 2004.

In late September 1965, a few days before the Seattle dates that produced *Om* and several other recordings, husband and wife Franzo and Marina King saw John Coltrane perform in San Francisco and were inspired to form a church centered on his music. They initially considered Coltrane a version of Christ then, during an alliance with Alice Coltrane, an avatar of Krishna (who is often depicted playing a flute), before they affiliated with the African Orthodox Church and recognized him as their patron saint.⁵⁶ The Saint John Will-I-Am Coltrane African Orthodox Church continues to meet regularly, with *A Love Supreme* and "Spiritual" central to services, both as recordings and performed live by the musician clergy.⁵⁷

On the other hand, as sales of *A Love Supreme* and *Karma* show, spiritual jazz has also been the most commercially successful free jazz. The clear and uplifting message and associated imagery are important factors, but specific musical aspects have also helped spiritual jazz cross over.

"The Creator Has a Master Plan" has three components: an "incantatory intro" where Sanders blows over held chords, an Afro-Cuban two-chord vamp, over which Leon Thomas sings the lyrics and improvises with Sanders, and a different, faster two-chord vamp, which resembles a gospel music shout section, during which Sanders and Thomas push the band to a series of extreme climaxes in which the rhythm section drops the vamp and joins in dense high-energy improvisation. However, when musicians, including Sanders and Thomas, perform "The Creator Has a Master Plan," it is frequently only the Afro-Cuban section.

The bass line is always present in this section, with only minor variations, and Thomas sings the title dozens of times. In contrast, during the first movement of *A Love Supreme*, Jimmy Garrison only repeats the bass line a few times as written to establish it before improvising, and the vocal chant appears for only a minute, following a substantial saxophone solo. Sanders presents the musical hooks early in the track and keeps them nearby, making his record much more accessible.

As on "Journey in Satchidananda," Sanders's playing on "The Creator Has a Master Plan" is closely inside the harmony. Almost every note is from a pentatonic scale matching the underlying chord. There are no substitutions, superimpositions, extensions, or other harmonic embellishments. Here the freedom of free jazz is the freedom to be sincere and direct, without the distance of sophistication. He is also free timbrally, pushing his tone up to the edge at the peaks of many phrases and completely over the edge in the ensemble climaxes.

This combination of pentatonic scales and sonic experimentation matched the vocabulary of many late 1960s rock guitarists, and Sanders's music connected in the nascent jam band and progressive rock scenes. Rock musicians had attempted to emulate John Coltrane's modal music on songs such as the Byrds' "Eight Miles High," the Doors' "Light My Fire," and the Butterfield Blues Band's "East-West;" Sanders offered a more accessible model for players and listeners, as shown by the dozens of cover versions of "The Creator Has a Master Plan."[58] Carlos Santana pays regular verbal and musical tribute to John Coltrane and collaborated with Alice Coltrane, but his versions of John Coltrane's music use repeating bass lines and straightforward pentatonic language much closer to Sanders. On *Love Devotion Surrender* (1973) he and John McLaughlin played the first movement of *A Love Supreme* over a Sanders-like vamp, as well as an arrangement of the traditional "Let Us Go into the House of the Lord" like that on Sanders's LP *Summun Bukmun Umyun*. Leon Thomas was even Santana's lead singer for a 1973 tour on which they performed "The Creator Has a Master Plan" and Sanders's "Japan," captured on the live album *Lotus*.

Bridge into the New Age

Like "Journey in Satachidananda," Sanders's late 1960s music was a version of what Alice Coltrane called a "unity concept," expressing universal spirituality through multicultural music. "The Creator Has a Master Plan" includes balafon, an assortment of shakers and bells, and harp-like strums inside the piano. Later pieces had similarly global instrumentation: "Village of the Pharoahs," from 1973, combined the saxophone, piano, bass, and drums jazz quartet with Indian tamboura, Japanese *shakuhachi*, and percussion from Africa and the Caribbean, to depict ancient Egypt.[59]

Sanders and Alice Coltrane's work also answers Amiri Baraka's call in his 1966 essay "The Changing Same" for a "unity music" combining the political and spiritual consciousness of free jazz with R and B's ability to communicate through lyrics and to connect listeners physically through embodied rhythms.[60] In the first half of the 1970s, this unity music manifested at intersections of multiple genres with a shared interest in groove-based improvisation. As in the case of *Karma*, this created some complex relationships between genres and between experimental and commercial music.

Argentine saxophonist Gato Barbieri's *The Third World*, recorded in November 1969, featured Sanders's pianist Lonnie Liston Smith along with Roswell Rudd on trombone, Charlie Haden on bass, and Beaver Harris on drums, veterans of Archie Shepp, Albert Ayler, and Ornette Coleman's bands. Barbieri and Rudd had played on Haden's *Liberation Music Orchestra* LP that April, which mixed Spanish Civil War songs, the civil rights anthem "We Shall Overcome," and compositions by Haden, Coleman, and Carla Bley, including an attempt to sonically represent the 1968 Democratic Convention through a structured improvisation.

On *The Third World*, Barbieri and his band play Brazilian, Argentine, and South African music as free jazz, taking the same rhythmic liberties that Rudd, Haden, and Harris had with swing, march, and funk rhythms backing Shepp on his *Mama Too Tight*. As on *Karma*, Smith creates drama and drive with big piano tremolos and clusters. Like Sanders, Barbieri has a full tone, wide vibrato, and tends to play either lyrical melodies or screaming.

While *Liberation Music Orchestra* had Haden, arranger and pianist Carla Bley, and a diverse band claiming a radical legacy from the Abraham Lincoln Brigade to the Yippies, *The Third World* used Barbieri's interpretations of South American music with a North American band to represent a general Latin American identity and the broader third world one of the title.[61] It employed many of the musical elements of spiritual jazz to construct an exoticized and politicized third world based on Barbieri's roots, analogous to other artists' versions of Africa and India. However, this was the apex of Barbieri's involvement with free jazz. He increasingly focused on delivering melodies over grooves, especially after his hit 1972 score to *Last Tango in Paris* and, from 1976's *Caliente!* onwards, he played Latin-flavored instrumental pop covers with little improvising. The albums between *The Third World* and *Caliente!* show an unexpected but logical path from spiritual jazz to smooth jazz, linked by valuing groove, atmosphere, and melody.

Drummer Norman Connors made his debut in 1967 on Archie Shepp's *The Magic of Ju-Ju*, in an Afro-Caribbean percussion section with Beaver Harris, Ed Blackwell, Frank Charles, and Dennis Charles. He played alongside Billy Hart on Pharoah Sanders's *Black Unity* and *Live at the East*, was the sole drum set player on Sanders's *Wisdom through Music*, *Love Is in Us All*, and some of *Village of the Pharoahs*, and also appeared on *Streams*, Sam Rivers's first record of free improvisation. For his own albums between 1972 and 1976, Connors called musicians connected to Sanders (Hart, bassists Cecil McBee and Stanley Clarke, saxophonists Gary Bartz and Carlos Garnett, and percussionists Lawrence Killian, Kenneth Nash, and Nat Bettis), Herbie Hancock (Hart, trumpeter Eddie Henderson, bassist Buster Williams, percussionist Bill Summers, and Hancock himself), and Miles Davis (Bartz, Garnett, guitarist Reggie Lucas, bass guitarist Michael Henderson, percussionists Airto Moriera and James Mtume Forman, and Billy Hart again). These players had multiple other notable connections. For example, McBee was the bassist on *Streams*, while Clarke and Airto were the original rhythm section of Chick Corea's Return to Forever. Although Hancock and Davis's music of the early 1970s shared spiritual jazz's interest in African, Indian, and Latin American sounds, in exploratory improvisation over repetitive bass-driven grooves, and in Black Power, pan-Africanism, and Afrofuturism, it employed a contrasting palette of electric and electronic sounds and streetwise attitudes drawn from inspirations such as James Brown, Sly Stone, Jimi Hendrix, and Funkadelic.[62]

The title track of Connors's 1972 *The Dance of Magic* opens with an "incantatory intro" similar to "The Creator Has a Master Plan" followed by a bass duet by McBee and Clarke leading into a fast one-chord Afro-Latin vamp close to what they had played a few months before on Sanders's *Black Unity*. They continue it under a pentatonic theme with a female vocal group singing the title, and then a series of solos. Everything stays in the groove; nothing gets too heated. It's essentially a smoother version of Sanders's music and is followed by "Morning Change," a straightforward mainstream Latin jazz song.

Connors continued to merge spiritual jazz and Black pop, culminating in a full-fledged slow jam version of "The Creator Has a Master Plan" on *You Are My Starship* in 1976. That album's title track, another slow jam, was a substantial hit, reaching number five on *Billboard*'s R and B chart, the apex of Connors's career. Both were sung by Michael Henderson, who began his career on bass guitar with Stevie Wonder then played with Miles Davis from 1971 to 1975.

James Mtume Forman played percussion with Davis throughout that period and also notably recorded with Pharoah Sanders on *Wisdom through Music* (1972) and *Love Is in Us All* (1973) and with Gato Barbieri on *Under Fire* (1971) and *Bolivia* (1973). Mtume's father was bebop saxophonist Jimmy Heath; his uncles were bassist Percy Heath and drummer Albert "Tootie" Heath. *Kawaida*, his debut album as a leader, was a tribute to the US Organization, a Los Angeles–based Black nationalist group led by Maulana Karenga. A pioneer of Afrocentrism now best known for popularizing Kwanza, Karenga promoted African-American liberation through the recovery of African identity and culture, in contrast to the Black Panthers' Marxist analysis.

Karenga's neo-African belief system gave *Kawaida* its title, and there are tracks named for him and for Amiri Baraka, who was his most prominent follower and advocate in the late 1960s.[63] Recorded in December 1969, *Kawaida* brought together Jimmy and Tootie Heath with Herbie Hancock, Hancock's regular bassist Buster Williams, and Ornette Coleman associates Don Cherry and Ed Blackwell. Sections of hand percussion and wooden flutes alternate with pentatonic melodies and modal vamps, and the musicians frequently chant or speak in Swahili, which Karenga promoted as a link to Africa. On the title track the musicians take turns defining, in English, Kawaida's seven principles, the *Nguzo Saba*: *Umoja* (unity), *Kujichagulia* (self-reliance), *Ujima* (collective work and responsibility), *Ujamaa* (cooperative economics), *Nia* (purpose), *Kuumba* (creativity), and *Imani* (faith).[64]

Cherry and Blackwell had recorded *Mu Parts 1 and 2*, two albums of multi-instrumental and multicultural duets, as part of the marathon BYG Actuel sessions in Paris in August and brought some of the spirit of that music to *Kawaida*. Cherry played piano on several *Mu* tracks, including two tributes to South African pianist Dollar Brand, and sections of *Kawaida* sound like either Cherry has taken over the piano bench or Hancock is emulating Cherry emulating Brand.

Mtume's second album as a leader, *Alkebu-Lan: Land of the Blacks (Live at the East)*, was recorded in August 1971. His Umoja Band drew from the same pool of musicians as Sanders, Davis, Hancock, Barbieri, and Connors, including Gary Bartz, Carlos Garnett, Buster Williams, Ndugu Chancler, and Billy Hart, and employed similar musical formulas.

His third album, 1977's *Rebirth Cycle*, added his Miles Davis comrades, guitarists Reggie Lucas and Pete Cosey, bass guitarist Michael Henderson, and drummer Al Foster.

Like Henderson, Lucas, and Norman Connors, Mtume also turned to pop songwriting. He and Lucas wrote Roberta Flack's 1978 number one R and B and number two pop hit single "The Closer I Get to You" and Stephanie Mills's 1980 Grammy-winner "Never Knew Love like This Before." The title track from *Juicy Fruit*, the third album by his eponymous R and B band, topped *Billboard*'s Hot Black Singles chart for eight weeks in the summer of 1983.

These stories do not necessarily show that Barbieri, Connors, or Mtume "sold out," or that Baraka's idea of "unity music" underestimated the recuperative powers of the music industry, but rather that multiple streams of Black music, as well as psychedelic and progressive rock, converged around combinations of deep grooves and post-Coltrane improvisation.[65]

Saxophonist Azar Lawrence began playing in Horace Tapscott's Pan-Afrikan People's Arkestra when he was in high school.[66] Tapscott's large ensemble performed mostly modal vamp–based music, including band members' compositions and arrangements of pieces by John Coltrane, Pharoah Sanders, McCoy Tyner, Stanley Cowell, and Charles Tolliver, often using several bassists, tuba, and multiple percussionists.[67] While much of this material relied on the pentatonic scales and fourths-based chords common in spiritual jazz, Tapscott's own compositions incorporated more dissonant harmony drawn from the clusters he often used in his piano playing and were frequently in odd or changing meters.[68] Deeply rooted in the African-American community in South Los Angeles, Tapscott and the Ark were connected to both the US Organization and the Los Angeles chapter of the Black Panthers despite the intense conflicts between those groups, and they accompanied Panther leader Elaine Brown on two albums of her songs.[69]

In the mid-1970s, Lawrence worked with the two surviving members of John Coltrane's classic quartet, recording with McCoy Tyner on *Enlightenment* (1973), *Sama Layuca* (1974), and *Atlantis* (1975), and with Elvin Jones on *New Agenda* (1975). He also made a guest appearance with Miles Davis at a 1974 Carnegie Hall concert released in Japan as *Dark Magus* and played on postbop trumpeter Woody Shaw's 1974 LP *The Moontrane*. At the same time, he recorded and toured with R and B artists including Marvin Gaye, Earth, Wind, and Fire, and Roberta Flack. His solo albums of the 1970s—*Bridge into the New Age* (1974), *Summer*

Solstice (1975), and *People Moving* (1976)—increasingly incorporate pop elements, in a trajectory similar to Barbieri, Connors, and Mtume. While jazz musicians have often worked in commercial music because of the high musicianship and low pay common in jazz, the genre convergence labeled "spiritual jazz" enabled Lawrence to take extended solos in mainstream jazz, free jazz, funk, fusion, and R and B contexts using a language based in John Coltrane's work up to 1965.

For example, on the song "Black Renaissance," which fills the first side of *Body, Mind, and Spirit*, a 1976 album led by keyboardist Harry Whitaker, who was the music director for Roberta Flack and Roy Ayers, Whitaker, Buster Williams, Billy Hart, and Mtume play a two-chord funk groove under long solos by Lawrence, Woody Shaw, and Whitaker himself, while echoey female voices laugh and say phrases like "What's happening?" and "It's time" at the far corners of the stereo field. Here spiritual jazz as a unity music links the most accessible elements of free jazz with the experimental side of R and B, but moving from R and B into jazz rather than the other direction.[70]

This is not music that has been freed from form; it is often more rhythmically and harmonically restricted than mainstream jazz, with unambiguous beats, repetitive bass lines, and limited chord movement. However, the trajectory of spiritual jazz from "Spiritual" to *A Love Supreme* to *Karma* to *Journey in Satchidananda* and onwards also shows a music freed to address the most profound topics, to employ materials from other cultures, and both to seek accessibility and to imagine going beyond entertainment or art to become a sacred activity: meditation, prayer, or ritual.

3

Energy

In the mid-1960s, free jazz musicians including Archie Shepp and Cecil Taylor, and the principal African-American critics interested in the new music—A. B. Spellman, Larry Neal, and Amiri Baraka—began discussing its form and aesthetics in terms of energy. For example, in a 1964 interview, Taylor said, "My music, contemporary music, mirrors inner energy."[1] Spellman's liner notes to John Coltrane's 1965 LP *Ascension* quoted Shepp describing it as based on "various fields of energy," and Baraka wrote in 1966 that "God is, indeed, energy. To play strong forever would be the cry and the worshipful purpose of life."[2] In 1968, Neal celebrated

> the kind of energy that informs the music of John Coltrane, Cecil Taylor, Albert Ayler, and Sun Ra—the modern equivalent of the ancient ritual energy. An energy that demands to be heard, and which no one can ignore. Energy to shake us out of our lethargy and free our bodies and our minds, opening us to unrealized possibilities.[3]

In the liner notes to *The New Wave in Jazz*, a record of a March 1965 concert he produced, Baraka wrote that Albert Ayler sees himself as "a vessel from which energy is issued."[4] Ayler's track on this album, "Holy Ghost," represents the techniques and aesthetics of energy in free jazz.[5] Its overall structure is simple and relatively standard: theme, solos by trumpet (Donald Ayler), tenor saxophone (Albert Ayler), cello (Joel

Freedman), and bass (Lewis Worrell), then the theme, a collective improvisation, and the theme once again. The theme is a seven-note phrase, consisting of a five-note scalar run up and down followed by a two-note cadence. On paper this figure clearly presents a four-beat measure and a major key, but as performed "Holy Ghost" has little if any connection to meter or tonality. Instead, the horns forcefully and irregularly pass the theme back and forth, introducing variations until the trumpet veers off into a solo. The players individually create and release energy without structural landmarks, chord changes, a rhythmic grid, or other external references to give their sounds meaning.[6] The strong forward momentum is not created by a relationship to set musical elements but by variations within the improvised lines, whether of pitch, volume, speed, timbre, or other qualities.[7] Bassist Barry Guy calls this "having a target:" each musical gesture moves toward its own point of emphasis.[8] Robert Sabin's transcription of Albert Ayler's and Gary Peacock's playing on "Ghosts" from Ayler's 1964 album *Spiritual Unity* makes visible this unsynchronized rise and fall.[9] Ekkehard Jost calls this "wave motion," like the infinite overlapping variations of the sea, and contrasts it to swing, which relies on the players' expressive relationship to a steady and shared pulse.[10]

Drummer Sunny Murray is largely responsible for replacing swing with wave. Murray was a working bebop drummer before he met Cecil Taylor, who encouraged him to "just play," directing him to "just let yourself play your drums, but listen too."[11] While some drummers explored extended technique and expanded setups, Murray largely retained the physical and instrumental configuration of bebop drumming: a very active right hand on the ride cymbal with divisions marked by the left foot on the hi-hat and punctuation from the right foot on the bass drum pedal and the left hand on the snare drum. His innovation was to detach this sonic vocabulary from the syntax of pulse, meter, and song form. As Taylor said, "The idea of the drum as a metronome is finished, and Sunny was one of the first drummers to realize that and develop a new approach."[12] Murray described learning in his first sessions with Taylor to

> not be hung up on artificial rules and roles and disciplines and orders that have been set up and which limit what you can express—or to be daring or hip while *still staying within the confines of those rules*, you know, like playing on one. He meant like to go outside of those rules and roles . . . to go outside of "time" and to play *naturally*—out of the *natural rules and*

rhythms of my body. Also to really listen to him to play *with* him, not just as an accompanist.[13]

Paul Bley considered this a logical successor to Ornette Coleman's break with song form and chord changes, what he called "the second revolution in jazz since 1957, the first abandoning tonality and the second abandoning time."[14] He explained:

> With Ornette, the bass player joined in the fray, but the drummer was *always* playing metronomic time—not necessarily four to the bar, but at least time. With the advent of Sunny Murray, Paul Motian, and Milford Graves, the drummer joined the bassist in the counterpoint. A lot of players managed to handle the absence of chord changes, although for many of them that was traumatic and still is. For myself, when the drummer gave up playing time, the music sounded totally different than it had the week before.[15]

Murray's constant motion was often too dense and irregular to create pulse or meter. Like the other members of the ensemble, he created energy through waves of activity. Amiri Baraka contrasted Murray to Tony Williams, whose work with Miles Davis and Eric Dolphy challenged the limits of timekeeping, writing, "Murray's intervals, his pulsations, are completely 'arbitrary.' Williams' only seem to be." He similarly emphasized that Murray's "accents are from immediate emotional necessity rather than the sometimes hackneyed demands of a pre-stated meter."[16] Williams brilliantly played with meter, pulse, and form, while Murray played without regard for those elements. Baraka's use of arbitrariness as a positive aesthetic quality, reflecting "immediate emotional necessity," is connected to the culture of spontaneity discussed earlier. It begs the question if a musician's spontaneous choice is more arbitrary than a composer's preestablished landmark, whether it is more arbitrary to accent a note because of "emotional necessity" or because it is the first beat of the third eight-bar section of a predetermined form.

Murray often mentioned Hermann von Helmholtz's 1863 book *On the Sensations of Tone*, a foundational work of musical acoustics. He was especially fascinated by the relationship between pulse and pitch: that a fast enough pulse becomes a tone, and the reverse. This manifested in his ride cymbal playing in particular, which blurred attacks and emphasized overtones, producing a constant drone. As he put it, "I was trying to get into the rapidity of beats to produce the sensation of tones."[17]

With Albert Ayler and in his own bands of the 1960s, Murray used his voice along with his drumming, groaning in harmony with his cymbal drone. His vocalizing also uses the wave motion of breath to embody the flow of energy. Improvisers such as George Benson and Slam Stewart sang along with their solos as an effect, but many more instrumentalists sing with themselves to enhance their phrasing. Brass and reed players are already governed by breath, but string, keyboard, and percussion players don't need to stop to breathe and can fall into mechanical, less expressive playing. Adding the voice encourages more human phrasing and articulations. This explains the more-or-less audible vocalizations of Bud Powell, Keith Jarrett, Karl Berger, Mark Dresser, Elvin Jones, Billy Higgins, and many others.[18]

While instrumental imitations of voices, such as bottleneck guitar and plunger-muted brass, have been part of jazz from the beginning, free jazz restored this to a central position and emphasized more extreme expressive registers. Amiri Baraka wrote in a concert review, "At the height of the music, the moaning and screaming came on in earnest. This is the ecstasy of the new music. At the point of wild agony or joy, the wild moans, screams, yells of life, in constant change."[19] By freeing the drums from timekeeping, Murray enabled them to phrase vocally, to produce sustained vocal-like sounds, and to merge with his actual voice.

On one level, as Paul Bley described, the break from the rhythmic grid into the energy music exemplified by "Holy Ghost" was simply the next move in freeing jazz after Ornette Coleman's break with song form. It tracked both the movement toward heightened abstraction, dissonance, and complexity characteristic of European modernism by eliminating a legible rhythmic framework and the postwar American culture of spontaneity by reducing the role of composition and premeditation. Gary Peacock fondly recalled Albert Ayler telling him the music "ain't about nothing," which Peacock took to mean that it didn't refer to anything outside itself, that it wasn't about race, politics, or identity, or about asserting or negating any particular musical concepts or material.[20] As Baraka wrote, Ayler "says he's not interested in note, he wants to play past note and get, then, purely into sound. Into the basic element, the clear emotional thing, freed absolutely from anti-emotional concept."[21] It is not only that the music isn't about the outside world, it also isn't about harmony or rhythm. One motive to free jazz was to free it from any impediments to immediate expression.[22]

There is a sequence in the documentary *My Name Is Albert Ayler* showing Peacock and Murray in the 2000s listening to their 1960s recordings with Ayler, laughing with joy.[23] However, free jazz in general and energy music in particular are often heard as representing anger because of the density, intensity, and physicality of the performances. Many musicians find this reductive and inaccurate. For example, multi-instrumentalist Cooper-Moore reconsidered the term "fire music," taken from the title of a 1965 Archie Shepp album: "Fire isn't anger either. You touch it, you feel it. It's just full of energy, it's full of energy. It's nothing bad," and pianist Marilyn Crispell told an interviewer:

> I have noticed that people tend to equate abstraction with negativity. Sometimes people'll say, oh I can really feel how angry you are when you play, and I look at them in amazement because I wasn't angry at all. They look at it in this very simplistic way, like you're playing something intense therefore you're expressing anger. I don't feel I'm expressing anger. I feel like I'm expressing energy, a moving energy that falls into certain patterns and rhythms, and all your experiences are in there—pain, anger, joy.[24]

However, at the risk of overelaborating a casual turn of phrase, the double negative of saying the music "ain't about nothing" also says that it isn't about nothing, that it is meaningful and consequential, "as serious as your life," as Valerie Wilmer entitled her book on free jazz.

The title "Holy Ghost" is not arbitrary. Albert Ayler was a deeply religious person and gave his pieces titles such as "Spirits," "Ghosts," "Angels," "Witches and Devils," "Truth Is Marching In," "Our Prayer," and "Light in Darkness." Many of the extreme effects he used on saxophone can be heard from gospel singers and saxophonists, and energy music can be understood ritualistically: the players manifest and channel the forces of the universe; the Holy Ghost enters worshippers who testify and speak in tongues until exhausted. Cooper-Moore recollects a Boston performance in the 1970s by the band Apogee, which included David S. Ware, Marc Edwards, and himself. Edwards played so intensely that he passed out and Ware and Cooper-Moore envied that he had reached that level.[25]

John Coltrane's piece "Ogunde" was an adaptation of the Afro-Brazilian folksong "Ogunde Varere," dedicated to Ogun, an orisha or spirit in the Yoruba religion. The band that played it on *The Olatunji Concert*, his April 1967 final recording, included Algie DeWitt playing the *batá* drum used in Yoruban observances and Cuban Santería. After a balladic introduction, they give an extremely energetic performance almost half an hour long, with John Coltrane, Pharoah Sanders, and Alice Coltrane all taking intense solos that embody the character of Ogun, the masculine warrior archetype. While free jazz is not Santería, this performance happens somewhere between a representation of spirit possession and the thing itself.[26] Albert Ayler's music has a similar relationship to ecstatic Christianity, as Amiri Baraka wrote:

> A saxophone, which was made by a German and played, as white folks call it, "legitimately," sounds like dead Lily Pons at a funeral, is changed by Ayler, or by members of any Sanctified or Holy Roller church (the blacker churches) into howling spirit summoner tied around the "mad" Black man's neck.[27]

It also matters that "Holy Ghost" was recorded at a benefit concert for Baraka's Black Arts Repertory Theater/School, held March 28, 1965, at the Village Gate. Baraka's career had exploded in 1964, with his plays *Dutchman*, *The Slave*, *The Toilet*, *The Eighth Ditch*, and *The Baptism* all produced in New York and widely reviewed, and *Dutchman* winning the Obie for Best American Off-Broadway Play. His second book of poems, *The Dead Lecturer*, appeared from Grove Press, and he was increasingly recognized as a public intellectual and racial spokesman, in demand as an essayist and speaker.

Baraka's rise paralleled Malcolm X's departure from the Nation of Islam and his increased political engagement. They often crossed paths and met for the last time in January 1965, for a long late-night conversation. According to Baraka, they discussed "introducing militancy into the Civil Rights Movement," while Allen Ginsberg remembered Baraka saying Malcolm had asked him to continue his work if anything happened to him.[28] When Malcolm X was assassinated February 21, Baraka left his family and creative community in Greenwich Village to move to Harlem and take up this charge. He announced the formation of the Black Arts Repertory Theater/School the next day. Albert Ayler,

Marion Brown, Giuseppi Logan, and Pharaoh Sanders performed at a fundraiser in the Village March 1, then Ayler, Sun Ra, John Coltrane, Archie Shepp, Grachan Moncur III, Charles Tolliver, and Betty Carter appeared at the Village Gate concert on the 28th.[29]

The initial publicity for the Black Arts Theater presented it as a school and showcase for Black actors, writers, and crew members, to help them enter the professional New York theater establishment.[30] However, when it opened in the summer of 1965, it was focused on revolutionary Black nationalist culture and politics. Members appeared to be preparing for armed struggle when it fell apart in early 1966.[31]

The nascent Black Arts and Black Power movements encompassed a wide range of ideologies and worldviews, as did the musical community, and performing at a fundraiser did not necessarily mean an artist endorsed a particular organization.[32] Baraka had personal and creative relationships with many of the new musicians, so they had many reasons to support his projects. When he lived in the Village, he and his family shared a building with Archie Shepp and Marzette Watts, which was just down the block from the Five Spot. Watts often hosted jam sessions and informal performances in his unit, and Marion Brown named a song on his first album for the address: 27 Cooper Square.[33] Baraka sometimes read his poetry at these sessions and appeared with Sunny Murray and the New York Art Quartet on their debut albums. His 1963 book *Blues People* and frequent contributions to *Downbeat*, *Metronome*, and other magazines established him as the leading African-American music writer of his time and the strongest interpreter and advocate of the new music.[34] Baraka's and A. B. Spellman's friendships and collaborations with musicians, including Shepp, Brown, Murray, and Watts, also marked the first time that jazz critics were true scene insiders.[35]

Much as the intensity of free jazz was read as anger, the music similarly became identified with Black radical politics. This was promoted in the mid-1960s by writers including Baraka and Frank Kofsky, who wrote, "Today's avant-garde movement in jazz is a musical representation of the ghetto's vote of 'no confidence' in Western civilization and the American Dream."[36] Musicians who articulated this connection include saxophonist Frank Lowe, who said, "The Black Panthers and Malcolm X—what these cats were saying and what we were listening to were all of the same mind," and violinist Billy Bang, who paralleled energy music and armed struggle:

> Musicians had no choice in the 1960s but to get into the political thing. A lot of the musicians did not have to get into the theoretical side of musicianship. . . . But they could pick up an instrument and it was like they were picking up an AK47. A lot of cats who were playing were picking up on the extensions of Coltrane. They did not study what made up a scale or the blues. They just started honking and screaming and the statements sounded like machine gun fire.[37]

Ascension

For the Black Arts Theater benefit recorded on *The New Wave in Jazz*, Coltrane and his regular quartet were joined by bassist Art Davis to play "Nature Boy," a song first popularized by Nat "King" Cole in 1948 whose modal melody and lyrical message of universal love matched Coltrane's musical and spiritual interests. Three months later this quintet recorded *Ascension*, joined by six horn players associated with the new music: alto saxophonists Marion Brown and John Tchicai, tenor saxophonists Pharoah Sanders and Archie Shepp, and trumpeters Freddie Hubbard and Dewey Johnson. Hubbard was the only one of these guests who came up through the mainstream. He had built a substantial discography with Art Blakey and as a leader by 1965 and had also appeared on avant-garde sessions including Eric Dolphy's *Out to Lunch* and Ornette Coleman's *Free Jazz*.

The form of *Ascension* is similar to *Free Jazz*: solos accompanied by the rhythm section alternating with full group improvisations. Each solo in *Ascension* begins with the rhythm section playing in time around B-flat minor, gradually breaks into energy playing, and ends when the other horns are cued in.[38] The overall structure resembles a religious service where participants take turns testifying, a form that is circular, moving around the group, rather than an arch, which starts small, builds to a climax, and winds back down.[39]

The sound of *Free Jazz* is much more open than *Ascension*; Coltrane's group was larger and louder. Coleman, Hubbard, Don Cherry, and Eric Dolphy carry on a conversation throughout *Free Jazz*, while the ensemble sections on *Ascension* create a wall of sound where individual contributions and interplay are difficult to pick out.[40] *Free Jazz* could be interpreted as a return to the polyphonic collective improvisations of New Orleans jazz, *Ascension* less so. This escalation of density is another major component of energy music and connects to several of the aesthetic streams feeding free jazz. In the liner notes to *Ascension*, Archie Shepp invoked Abstract Expressionism: "The idea is similar to what the action painters do in that it creates various surfaces of color which push into each other, creates tensions and counter tensions, and various fields of energy," while Amiri Baraka elsewhere linked Coltrane, Ayler, and Sun Ra's embrace of all-out group improvising to an essential and spiritual Blackness, writing, "The return to collective improvisations, which finally, the West-oriented, the whitened, say, is chaos, is the *all-force* put together, and is what is wanted."[41]

A. B. Spellman's liner notes to *Ascension* celebrated it as a brutal sublime, stating that "it begins on a level at which most performances end and moves to a higher plane than the average listener considers comfortable" that, after listening, "your nervous system has been dissected, overhauled, and reassembled," and that Coltrane attempts "to empty his own and his audience's spiritual reservoir."[42] This experience of being overwhelmed and exhausted by a work of art is new to jazz. Paul Hegarty links this aspect of free jazz to the growing role of noise in twentieth century music and the emergence of noise as a genre. He writes that *Ascension* "disrupts cognitive listening, and its duration is itself a force."[43] The piece "drains the audience's spiritual reservoir" by pushing the limits of their attention and endurance.

Sun Ra described using noise as a kind of musical Theater of Cruelty to raise listeners' consciousness:

> I like all the sounds that upset people, because they're too complacent, and there are some sounds that really upset them, and man, you need to shock them out of their complacency, 'cause it's a very bad world in a lot of aspects. They need to wake to how bad it is, then maybe they'll do something about it.[44]

However, transgression is also part of the appeal of noise in music and noise as music. Sun Ra described this as well, mentioning a fan who said he came to see Ra "'cause you *abuse* the piano," repeating for emphasis that the man "wanted to see a piano *abused*."[45] Poet Ted Joans famously compared Albert Ayler's saxophone sound to someone "screaming the word 'FUCK' in Saint Patrick's Cathedral on crowded Easter Sunday."[46] These stories of Black men violating icons of Western civilization, whether a Steinway or a Catholic mass, are charged with sex and violence, and the knowing listener has the pleasure of identifying both with the shocking performer and those shocked.

Jazz is often celebrated as a democratic music in which creative individuals freely join together and negotiate between individualism and interconnectedness.[47] However, this kind of subjectivity breaks down in the ensemble passages of *Ascension* and similar large group improvisations. It becomes extremely difficult to tell who is playing what and what each musician plays matters less as it blurs into a roar. A line is crossed from community to collective. This may be part of what Baraka meant when he concluded his liner notes to *The New Wave in Jazz*, "New Black Music is this: Find the self, then kill it."[48]

Machine Gun

In the late 1960s *Ascension*-style energy playing was embraced by a network of European musicians centered in Germany. As saxophonist Peter Brötzmann, one of the main nodes in this network, said, "1968 was the year of the big groups, where we met friends in order to play like madmen," referring to Manfred Schoof's *European Echoes*, Alexander von Schlippenbach's *The Living Music*, and his own album *Machine Gun*.[49] Brötzmann and bassist Peter Kowald dubbed this the "kaputtspiel phase."[50] *Kaputtspiel* literally translates to "broken play" and connotes the demolition of existing rules and standards. As Kowald put it, "In certain revolutionary phases, conventions get destroyed and traditions negated, and then something new can come into existence."[51] Ekkehard Jost listed typical aspects of the music on these records:

- limited, simple, or ironic composed material
- density and volume replace pitch as the main organizational elements
- a tendency toward extremes
- "a diffuse and intense totality" rather than individual lines
- little audible development
- relentless motion, with implied tempos often around 300BPM

- personal and often nontraditional instrumental technique
- a German/British/Dutch network of players[52]

Kowald also called this the "kill the fathers" stage of European free music.[53] This had several meanings. Germans coming of age in the 1960s had to reckon with the Nazi period. As Brötzmann explained, "Our fathers left us with so many unanswered questions after the war. We wanted to destroy everything out fathers stood for."[54] His own father had been forced to join the Wehrmacht.[55] More generally, after the Third Reich German national and cultural identity was an utterly undesirable patrimony. Brötzmann saw free jazz as offering liberation from the burden of German history.[56]

However, the United States, American musicians, and jazz itself were also metaphorical fathers to be killed.[57] While Brötzmann described his connection to jazz as "a way to be on the right side in the war between the poor and the rich, the black and the white," European youth movements of the 1960s reacted against American hegemony, the rising nuclear threat of the Cold War, and the escalating conflict in Vietnam.[58] Jazz was part of American mass culture, a capitalist product, and a vector of cultural imperialism.

With the notable exception of guitarist Django Reinhardt, European jazz musicians had historically relied on imitating American examples.[59] This particularly characterized the initial dissemination of free jazz in France. French free players identified with Albert Ayler's aesthetic transgressions, which they connected to European art movements such as Dada, but they failed to recognize the ecstatic spirituality at the center of his music.[60] Saxophonist/clarinetist Michel Portal recorded with Sunny Murray in late 1968 and led his own Ayler-inspired album, *Our Meanings and Our Feelings*, the next summer. At the time, Portal both described himself as "becoming Black" when he played free jazz and recognized that he was appropriating Black music.[61]

A significant number of European players came to a different conclusion from Brötzmann or Portal: rather than joining or copying African-American free jazz, they took it as a model of innovation instead of a set of musical practices and attempted to make music of their own that was as unique and personal as Coleman's, Coltrane's, and Ayler's. The German jazz critic and Berlin Jazz Festival organizer Joachim-Ernst Berendt called this search for distinctively European creative music "the

Emancipation."[62] As Dutch pianist Misha Mengelberg said, "The music we play, we and the other European musicians, even those who invoke 'free jazz,' has no longer anything to do with Afro-American music. But we are inspired, it must be acknowledged, by this music in order to create our own."[63] Drummer Han Bennink, Mengelberg's partner in the Instant Composers Pool and a frequent Brötzmann collaborator, said in 1971:

> I play a European music. Five or six years before, we could hear musicians in Europe that were repeating what the Blacks were saying, that were stealing their music and the results were quite sad. Nowadays, and I'm happy about that, I have nothing to do with Americans anymore. They have a musical background that only belongs to them.[64]

Guitarist Keith Rowe, of the British group AMM, explained: "Black musicians had invented a new kind of music—jazz, and we wanted to do that, but we were skinny white European kids, young men, and what did that mean? We wanted to make a form of music which had never existed before in the history of music."[65] Because free jazz questioned every musical convention, including those of jazz, it could simultaneously be a platform for this radical exploration and another father to be killed.

While the Emancipation was driven by a search for artistic freedom and authentic personal voices and a desire to not appropriate the innovations of African-American musicians, it also risked unifying European improvisation around whiteness and elevating that identity. British drummer Tony Oxley said in 1974, "The most aggressive, potent avant-garde black group still has the swing element in it, and it's the element that's holding them back."[66] Berendt might not have associated the word "emancipation" with the Emancipation Proclamation and the liberation of African-Americans from slavery, but the irony of using it to describe European improvising musicians discarding African-American musical influences is intense.[67] Kowald, Oxley, and Brötzmann later collaborated with African-American free jazz players including Fred Anderson, Anthony Braxton, Andrew Cyrille, Bill Dixon, Hamid Drake, Charles Gayle, Milford Graves, Julius Hemphill, Fred Hopkins, Ronald Shannon Jackson, Jeanne Lee, George Lewis, Joe McPhee, William Parker, Sonny Sharrock, Cecil Taylor, and David S. Ware, but in the early 1970s the rhetoric of the Emancipation risked implying that jazz was being freed from its Blackness.

Brötzmann was the central figure of the kaputtspiel phase and the Emancipation. He and Han Bennink were the only musicians who appeared on all three of *European Echoes*, *The Living Music*, and *Machine Gun*, and he and Jost Gelbers established two essential parts of the European free jazz and free improvisation scene, starting the annual Total Music Meeting festival in 1968 and the Free Music Productions record label the next year.[68] However, Brötzmann rejected the premise of the Emancipation and saw his music as essentially connected to African-American free jazz, explaining, "There was a time in Europe when a lot of musicians, and especially the English guys, said: 'Fuck the Americans, we're doing our own stuff.' I always said, 'no man, I like that way of playing.'"[69] His version of this "way of playing" helped define the kaputtspiel phase. His 1967 debut album *For Adolphe Sax* was the first self-produced European jazz record and the first German record of free improvisation, possibly the first European one.[70] It continues a line from Albert Ayler's 1965 release *Spiritual Unity* through *The Frank Wright Trio* from 1966: each further deconstructs the tenor saxophone, bass, and drums trio, reducing the roles of composition, conventional musical elements, and instrumental technique, and increasing those of energy and noise.[71] As Brötzmann said, "We were fed up with harmony and bars and counting and forms, we had the will to go as far out as possible."[72]

For Adolphe Sax was the first recording of Brötzmann, Kowald, and drummer Sven-Åke Johansson. Like Ornette Coleman, they had not proven their skills in mainstream jazz before presenting themselves as free players and, as when Coleman began playing trumpet and violin and working with his child Denardo on drums, they defied conventional ideas of instrumental proficiency. The album's title invokes the history of the saxophone, asking what its inventor would have thought of the art made with his creation, but it also erases that history: Brötzmann often seems to approach the saxophone with little regard for existing ideas on how it should be played. German critics recognized Brötzmann's "incompetence" as an artistic choice like Coleman's, a refusal to play properly rather than a failure. Defining the aesthetics of the kaputtspeil phase, they also described it as "vitality" turning into "brutality" and called him "a demonaic satyr."[73] British saxophonist Evan Parker, who appeared on *Machine Gun*, said, "Brötzmann is about pure sound and energy through the saxophone, he's just a force of nature through the saxophone," and described the experience of playing with him: "Quite often we ended up with blood, it was a messy business some nights."[74]

Machine Gun, recorded in May 1968, the month of the Paris student/worker protests, has come to represent a pinnacle of aggressive, noisy playing, what David Toop calls "a benchmark of the fiercest imaginable energy."[75] Brötzmann took the title from a nickname Don Cherry gave him, which was inspired by his playing, but he also put an image of a soldier with a machine gun on the cover.[76] The title track begins with the three tenor saxophonists blasting their lowest pitch in short, even, repeated notes, imitating the sound of automatic gunfire, embracing Billy Bang's metaphor.

A number of free jazz compositions use noise programmatically or onomatopoetically. Sun Ra regularly cued "space chords" by raising both his arms, directing the band to sustain any note at maximum volume, creating a wall of sound that could represent the terrifying emptiness of space and also annihilated whatever previous sounds or thoughts might have been in the listeners' heads. Similarly, the textures of the massive pieces Alan Silva created with his Celestrial Communications Orchestra were specifically representational. For *Luna Surface*, the overtone-rich drone stood for the surface of the moon and the moon's spiritual meanings, while, in *Seasons*, "the mass ending is about Vietnam, about being in the jungle, with trills. This, to me, is a jungle warfare piece."[77]

Machine Gun is not a spontaneous eruption. Over the course of fifteen minutes the title track includes numerous planned events and even some composed elements. *Free Jazz* and *Ascension* essentially alternated solo and group passages, with each soloist accompanied by the rhythm section and the other horns free to converse, but, with two bassists, two drummers, and piano available, "Machine Gun" varies the rhythm section configuration for each soloist and gives the horns fresh material to play under each solo. After the initial machine gun motif, Evan Parker has the first solo, accompanied by piano, one bassist, and one drummer, interrupted by cued ensemble blasts on a single pitch. Fred Van Hove follows on piano, with both bassists and drummers and cued ascending lines from the horns, then there is a bowed bass duet with percussion accompaniment. The entire group reenters with a slow upward climb that turns into a scream at its peak. Willem Breuker's bass clarinet solo begins unaccompanied, then is joined by the full rhythm section. The other horns enter with a short written melody that becomes a group freakout, followed by a slow descent in pitch and volume that mirrors the climb that launched the solo. Brötzmann solos last, also with the full rhythm section. The other horns return with a unison riff straight from a Stax R and B record, the drums move from energy playing to join them with a backbeat, then the ensemble accelerates into chaos and concludes with the machine gun motif.[78] This last climax is difficult to read in the context of the Emancipation, since it overtly invokes American popular culture, albeit African-American popular culture. Why did Brötzmann use a pop music moment for the apex of this piece? It seems just as credible to hear it connecting free jazz to R and B, as a found object, and as gunning down American pop: Brötzmann as post-Ayler improviser, post-Pop artist, and May '68 revolutionary.

The mystique of this record, along with Brötzmann's consistently intense performances, provocative album titles (e.g., *Nipples* and *Balls*), and matching graphic design style, helped link free jazz to punk and metal. In 1996, Sonic Youth guitarist and record collector Thurston Moore published an influential list of his top ten free jazz albums, seemingly chosen for rarity and noise value. Moore selected *Nipples* over *Machine Gun*, possibly because the later was still in print, but called *Machine Gun* "the most mind-blasting" European improvisation record, and "a smashing clanging wonderland of noise."[79] Punk, metal, and noise overlap aesthetically with the kaputtspiel in valuing raw performances, speed, volume, density, and iconoclastic approaches to musical history, form, and technique.

Detroit protopunks the MC5 may have been the first rock band to make this connection. In the late 1960s, they embraced free jazz as a model of cathartic noise, performed Sun Ra and Pharoah Sanders covers, and shared bills with Ra's Arkestra.[80] This sensibility has since manifested in free jazz/rock/noise collaborations and crossovers such as Last Exit (Brötzmann with Sonny Sharrock, Bill Laswell, and Ronald Shannon Jackson), John Zorn groups including Painkiller (with Laswell and Napalm Death drummer Mick Harris), Robert Musso's aptly named band Machine Gun (which often included Sharrock), the Lounge Lizards' first LP, power trios Harriet Tubman and Power Tools, Black Flag's instrumental album *The Process of Weeding Out*, LA jazz/punk groups Universal Congress Of and Cruel Frederick, the electric guitar-focused explorations of Eugene Chadbourne, Elliott Sharp, Nels Cline, Henry Kaiser, and Ava Mendoza, among others, projects by Sonic Youth, including their 2003 collaboration with Swedish free jazz saxophonist Mats Gustafsson and Japanese electronic noise artist Merzbow, Gustafsson's trio the Thing, and many more.

We Now Create

Like the Europeans, Japanese jazz musicians had historically relied heavily on American models while negotiating the challenge of making music that was both distinctively their own and connected to jazz's African-American roots.[81] This became increasingly difficult as musicians and critics identified jazz more explicitly with the Black experience, particularly through the gospel and funk references of hard bop and the radical politics of free jazz.[82]

Initially, the trio co-led by bassist Motoharu Yoshizawa and saxophonist Mototeru Takagi emulated Coleman and Ayler, fitting Japanese scales and folk melodies and archetypically Japanese inspirations such as miso soup and the sea into their models.[83] However, by May 1969, when Yoshizawa and Takagi joined guitarist Masayuki Takayanagi in drummer Masahiko Togashi's quartet for the album *We Now Create*, these references were abandoned in pursuit of unique personal voices.[84] This LP tied for Album of the Year in the Japan Jazz prizes and was considered the arrival of Japanese free jazz.[85] Like *For Adolphe Sax*, it eschews composition, tonality, and a rhythmic grid, with coherence created entirely by the performers' will.

Japanese jazz critic and concert organizer Tetsuo Teruto claims "jazz really became 'indigenous' everywhere when it became free jazz," citing the contributions of the German Brötzmann and Dutch Han Bennink as well as those of his own countrymen.[86] At the same time that free jazz was specifically linked to African-American politics, spirituality, and identity, freeing jazz from song form, tonality, countable time, and other musical prescriptions, repertoire, or technical requirements enabled others to use it as a platform. The more open the form, the more possible it becomes for a wider range of voices to participate. *We Now Create* is a paraphrase of *This Is Our Music*.

Like the Emancipation, Teruto's claim that free jazz became an international style risks detaching the music from its sources, seeing Blackness as one of the conventions jazz needed to be freed from, but numerous collaborations that center African-American artists, such as Michel Portal's 1969 work with Sunny Murray and Milford Graves's 1977 album *Meditation Among Us*, with an all-Japanese band including Mototeru Takagi, suggest otherwise. In 1991 Peter Kowald, who twenty years before had been an outspoken advocate of the Emancipation, released a set of three LPs of improvised duos, one with Europeans, one with Americans, and one with Japanese musicians.

4

Experimentalism

Completely improvised performances such as *For Adolphe Sax*, *Om*, *We Now Create*, and Kowald's *Duos* represent a significant direction opened by freeing jazz. With composition, form, harmony, and rhythm optional or open to real-time negotiation, it was possible for work to be created without composition or planning, for musicians to "just play," as Cecil Taylor directed Sunny Murray. Many artists adopted this approach for specific pieces and projects or as their central practice.

After working briefly with Miles Davis in 1964, Sam Rivers joined the community of progressive jazz players recording on Blue Note, leading his own sessions and appearing on albums by Bobby Hutcherson, Tony Williams, Larry Young, and Andrew Hill. In 1969, he toured with Cecil Taylor then began focusing on entirely improvised music, usually with a trio. The first documentation of this approach was *Streams*, recorded at the 1973 Montreux Jazz Festival.

Although Rivers's performances were spontaneous, they had a consistent overall structure with segments devoted to each of his four instruments: soprano and tenor saxophones, piano, and flute. The sequence varied between shows (on *Streams*, it is tenor, flute, piano, and soprano), but Rivers seldom alternated instruments or revisited one.

The audience bursts into applause around twelve and a half minutes into *Streams* when, after moving between incantatory and energy playing, the trio locks into a medium-fast swing. This breaks down and resumes several times before bassist Cecil McBee picks up his bow to conclude the tenor segment. Drummer Norman Connors begins a solo, with

McBee strumming chordal punctuation, and Rivers's shouts and yelps lead the band into his voice and flute segment. This passes through a faster swing feel and, during the first few minutes of the second LP side, a funky vamp. The concluding soprano saxophone segment includes both funk and fast swing areas, then the group begins looking for an ending.

Rivers's trios interpreted freedom as "freedom to" rather than "freedom from." The absence of predetermined grooves, tonalities, or compositions did not mean the band only played out of time, atonally, or without melody. Instead, the musicians were free to propose, support, and subvert tempos, tonalities, and themes, as well as references to established musical styles such as swing and funk.[1] As bassist Dave Holland, a frequent Rivers collaborator, put it, "Sam's thing was wide open, we never played a note of music that was written in the small group. Sam used to say, play all the music, play vamps, play free, play everything."[2]

Rivers and his band members create coherence in free playing with targeted recurring notes, melodic imitation, shared pulse, and shared meter. McBee moves between "time, no changes," modal walking, drones, riffs built on the minor pentatonic (also known as "the blues scale"), and atonal counterpoint. The group also consciously returns to specific areas during a performance, as when the swing feel stops and starts during the tenor saxophone section of *Streams*.[3] While their work is completely spontaneous, it is also idiomatic; they create primarily through and around jazz conventions about time, groove, tonality, and structure.

Imaginary Values

Guitarist Derek Bailey, saxophonist Evan Parker, and trombonist Paul Rutherford were the most active British participants in the German/Dutch/British network of the kaputtspiel era: Bailey played on Peter Brötzmann's *Nipples* and Manfred Schoof's *European Echoes*, Rutherford was on *European Echoes* and Alexander von Schlippenbach's *The Living Music*, and Parker was on *Machine Gun* and *European Echoes*. Bailey and Parker launched their Incus Records label in 1970 with a trio album with Han Bennink entitled *The Topography of the Lungs*, and all three appeared in various combinations on early releases on Bennink, Willem Breuker, and Misha Mengelberg's Instant Composers Pool label.

Unlike their continental associates, the British players tended to refuse musical conventions rather than loudly defy them. As Ekkehard Jost put it, British free music was "more ascetic than ecstatic."[4] Parallel to the Emancipation in European free music, Bailey advanced the idea of "non-idiomatic" improvisation. As bassist Simon H. Fell describes it, nonidiomatic improvisation has no predetermined elements and avoids references to other music.[5] While Bailey, Parker, and Rutherford developed instantly recognizable personal musical vocabularies, they did not formulate a grammar for the new music; the terms of the relationships of sounds and players within a performance were always in flux. On *Streams*, when Sam Rivers played a scale fragment, he was suggesting to Cecil McBee that they play in that tonality for a while, and when McBee set a groove he was inviting Norman Connors to join him. In nonidiomatic playing, those gestures do not carry those implications and the other musicians remain free to respond however they like, including not reacting. If they choose to connect, it is not in relation to preexisting ideas such as tonality or groove.

At some point, this music stops being jazz. Some British improvisers, such as Bailey and the members of AMM, while remaining jazz fans, took a version of the Emancipation as a premise of their work: genres and styles are idioms.[6] Evan Parker's trio with bassist Barry Guy and drummer Paul Lytton often has the drive of energy music but also pushes towards a nonidiomatic deconstruction of musical language.[7] This trio developed from Parker's duo with Lytton, which formed in 1969. Each initially used a wide range of sound-making devices, including homemade instruments and reel-to-reel tapes of their past performances, and their work paralleled the electroacoustic experiments of underground improvising groups such as AMM and the Music Improvisation Company (which included Parker and Bailey) and of classical musicians working with electronics and improvisation such as Karlheinz Stockhausen, Musica Elettronica Viva, Gruppo di Improvvisazione Nuova Consonanza, and Gentle Fire, much more than free jazz. These formations overlapped: Cornelius Cardew of AMM and Hugh Davies, a member of both the Music Improvisation Company and Gentle Fire, worked as Stockhausen's assistants in the 1960s, while Karl Berger, Steve Lacy, George Lewis, and Anthony Braxton performed with MEV.[8]

Parker and Lytton increasingly focused on their primary instruments as the 1970s progressed. Around 1980, Parker played a duo with Barry Guy and decided to merge the two duos into a trio.[9] Ending up with the classic saxophone, bass, and drums trio instrumentation in this roundabout way implies Parker, Guy, and Lytton's ambivalent relationship to the jazz tradition. Asked if his music was jazz, Parker replied he saw jazz as a spectrum. The trio negotiates its proximity to jazz from performance to performance and from moment to moment.[10]

"Form," the opening track on their 1994 album *Imaginary Values*, begins with seven minutes of high energy free playing in the Ayler/Wright/Brötzmann lineage. Lytton then switches from a chattering post–Sunny Murray free jazz style to bowing, rubbing, scraping, and using other extended techniques on the drums and cymbals. Parker uses extreme articulations, key clicks, and attenuated dynamics, while Guy often plays in the upper register of the bass, attacks the strings with various implements, jams objects between the strings, and uses a volume pedal to alter the attacks and decays of notes. These percussive approaches to the saxophone and bass intersect with techniques for producing more sustained and pitched sounds from the drums and cymbals to blur the boundaries between the instruments. The instruments often share the same register and timbral qualities, erasing expectations that one would lead and the others accompany, that one would emphasize melody and the others rhythm, and so on.[11] Even expert listeners cannot always tell who is making which sound, or how.

Parker, Guy, and Lytton have been a working group for over thirty years with a dozen albums as a trio, several with added guests, and at least another dozen as the core of Parker's Electro-Acoustic Ensemble and Guy's New Orchestra. Experimental rock musician Jim O'Rourke once commented that the Parker/Guy/Lytton trio didn't improvise but "played Evan Parker trio music." Asked about this, Parker embraced the proposition that the rapport developed through the trio's long-term collaboration was its own idiom.[12]

Sound Structure of Subculture Becoming

In 1965, Cecil Taylor told an interviewer:

> If a man plays for a certain amount of time . . . eventually a kind of order asserts itself. Whether he chooses to notate that personal order or engage in polemics about it, it's there. That is, if he's saying anything in his music. There is no music without order—if that music comes from a man's innards.[13]

Freeing jazz encouraged artists to seek, notate, and articulate their personal concepts of order, whether they originated in theory or practice. As Taylor put it, "The thing that makes jazz so interesting is that each man is his own academy. By and large, if he's really going to be persuasive, he learns about other academies, but the idea is that he must have that special thing."[14] His own system emerged in the first half of the 1960s, as he stopped playing song forms and countable time and began organizing his music around what have become known as "unit structures" after his 1966 LP.

Taylor's liner notes to *Unit Structures*, a long poetic essay entitled "Sound Structure of Subculture Becoming Major Breath/Naked Fire Gesture," are the closest he came to explaining his aesthetics or methods. They list three types of musical event: "anacrusis," "plain," and "area." Although he seems to have rarely used these specific terms outside of this text, they help describe the large-scale elements of his music. In general, in music an anacrusis is a preparatory gesture, such as a conductor's upbeat to indicate the tempo before the first played beat or notes played as pickups to a downbeat, while in poetry it is the equivalent of pickup notes: syllables before the first beat of a line's meter. Taylor's compositions often begin with short repeated figures, which are an anacrusis to the longer melodic phrases that make up the plain, and the areas, which are improvisational spaces. On the title track of *Unit Structures*, the first minute is an anacrusis, the next four a melodic plain, and the five following an area with solos by Ken McIntyre on bass clarinet and Jimmy Lyons on alto saxophone.[15]

Taylor eschewed conventional notation, teaching his material in fragments by demonstrating it on piano or by dictating note names. His musicians jotted the note names down as letters, sometimes in the rising and falling contours of the melody, and he adopted this himself. The first phrase of "Happy Birthday" would be written C C D C F E in this notation. These melodic cells are the "units" of the unit structures approach. Taylor and his players usually state them at least once in their basic form, often in a rough unison, but improvised elaborations are always possible in all three types of sections. Players are free to invert or reverse the melodic shape and to reorder, repeat, add, or replace notes. They can also approach a unit as intervals rather than pitches, so that first phrase of "Happy Birthday" could be understood as a whole step up and down followed by a fourth up and a half step down, and these intervals can be treated as freely as the pitches.[16]

Taylor's system is a starting point, not a limit; new material can always be introduced.[17] He chose strongly individualistic players for his bands and expected them to bring their own personalities and ideas. As

Jimmy Lyons, Taylor's collaborator from 1961 to 1984, said, "He has scales, patterns, and tunes that he uses, and the soloist is supposed to use these things. But you can take it out. If you go into your own thing, Cecil will follow you there."[18]

Taylor avoided attaching his music to a rhythmic grid. As he put it, "A student asked me once where the pulse is in my music. I asked him how many different rates of breathing there are. I told him that what I'm interested in in my music is the variety of pulses that exist in a given moment."[19] As in Jost's idea of wave motion, there are potentially as many simultaneous rhythmic planes as there are performers, and each of them can vary expressively.[20]

Performers are also free to sequence, layer, and overlap the units, creating polyphony, arrangement, and orchestration in performance. Taylor told one ensemble, "We will decide how the sounds please us, and we will develop them as we go along."[21] This rhythmic and structural freedom often generated extremely energized performances and obscured the substantial role of composition in Taylor's music, to the degree that some believe it was "all but completely improvised."[22] The opposite seems to be true. Sam Rivers said the music he played with Taylor was almost all composed, by which he surely meant they were interpreting the pitch/interval units.[23] Taylor also used the anacrusis/plain/area and unit structures concepts when playing solo, as well as in completely spontaneous settings; he did not separate his compositional and improvisational processes.[24]

It can be easier to hear the role of pitch/interval units on albums by Taylor's associates who have adopted his system, such as Jimmy Lyons, Glenn Spearman, and Marco Eneidi, than in his own work. Taylor's piano playing is often so dense and pushes the rest of the band so hard that the compositional logic is overwhelmed. This was almost certainly intentional. Taylor repeatedly disdained authoring and presenting compositions as a goal, declaring, "I don't think I would ever want to be considered a composer," and that "to sit down and write a piece of music and to ask musicians to perform that music under the same directorial tutelage that Handel gave his musicians, seems to me to be rather questionable in concept."[25] Instead, his compositions and system are designed to exceed themselves. As Lyons said, Taylor encouraged his musicians to improvise both with the material and beyond it. Taylor described his music as driven by "religious forces" and the frequent references to Aztec and Yoruba spiritual figures and concepts in his titles and poems signal his transcendent intentions.[26]

Ankhrasmation

Trumpeter Wadada Leo Smith made his debut on Anthony Braxton's *Three Compositions of New Jazz*, recorded and released in 1968. Although the album was credited to Braxton, it was the work of their collective trio with violinist Leroy Jenkins: the Creative Construction Company. This group was often augmented by pianist Muhal Richard Abrams, as on this album, or drummer Steve McCall.[27]

Smith, Braxton, Jenkins, Abrams, and McCall were all members of the AACM, a cooperative of African-American musicians in Chicago organized by Abrams, McCall, pianist Jodie Christian, and former Sun Ra trumpeter Philip Cohran in May 1965.[28] The AACM supported original music exclusively and organized performances by their members outside of the expectations and limitations of the nightclub format.

Three Compositions of New Jazz was the fifth AACM album, following Roscoe Mitchell's *Sound*, Joseph Jarman's *Song For*, Abrams's *Levels and Degrees of Light*, and Lester Bowie's *Numbers 1 & 2*. The music on all these albums emphasized a variety of individual sounds and collective textures in place of swinging grooves or dense energy playing. This reflected the AACM's encouragement of multi-instrumentalism and solo performance.

Multi-instrumentalism in jazz had primarily been a way to bring different colors to a consistent role. A saxophone player might play a song on flute or clarinet or switch from tenor to soprano but stay a melodic soloist, just as a bassist might switch to tuba or bass guitar or a pianist to an electric piano or synthesizer but play the same role in the rhythm section. Secondarily, horn players might pick up shakers, cowbells, and other hand percussion during a Latin or other groove-based piece, whether in Duke Ellington's band or Pharoah Sanders's.

Smith's concept is different, as he wrote in his book *Notes (8 Pieces) Source a New World Music*:

> The new creative musician in most cases would be multi-instrumentalist, but for other creative musicians this would not be necessary, *for the instrument is only part of a larger consciousness that transcends the mere means of an instrument or instruments*— what is required is that the new creative improvisor must have the absolute ability to instantaneously organize sound, silence, and rhythm with the whole of his or her creative intelligence.

Becoming a "new creative musician" includes assembling a personal sonic palette. In this context, not only is a bicycle horn as valid as a saxophone, but they both become parts of what Smith calls "one complete instrument."[29]

On "Nine (9) Stones on a Mountain," the first track on his first album as a leader, Smith performs solo using "trumpet, seal horn, recorder, Indian wooden flute, harmonica, autoharp, hand zithers, bells." It opens and closes with a composed trumpet melody. For the improvisation, Smith moves quickly through his other pitched instruments, playing a phrase or two on each using material from the theme while simultaneously rustling or striking various small percussion instruments. Almost exactly halfway through the track, he doubles a trumpet phrase with the seal horn, which is a three-pitched version of a bicycle horn that a trained seal might play with its nose. Although the trumpet is the frame and center of this piece, the improvisation on "Nine (9) Stones on a Mountain" is a truly multi-instrumental performance.

His AACM peers were working along similar lines. Roscoe Mitchell's 1967 "Solo" begins with a phrase on his primary instrument—the alto saxophone—but, like Smith's piece, it proceeds through exchanges between other elements of his "complete instrument": dinner bells, assorted gongs, harmonica, and clarinet. Unlike "Nine (9) Stones on a Mountain," "Solo" features a substantial solo improvisation on Mitchell's primary instrument, and it may not have any precomposed material. Although the alto saxophone sections focus on a repeated phrase, it may have been spontaneously developed.[30]

Freeing musicians to use their choice of instruments and ultimately to make any sound at any time alters the relationship of players within an ensemble. As Smith wrote:

> The concept that I employ in my music is to consider each performer as a complete unit with each having his or her own center from which each performs independently of any other, and with this respect of autonomy the independent center of the improvisation is continually changing depending upon the force created by individual centers at any instance from any of the units.[31]

This autonomy does not preclude using composed material, as the theme to "Nine Stones" shows, or arrangements, as on Smith and Marion Brown's recording of Brown's "And They Danced," where each in turn plays the simple melody on his primary instrument while the other accompanies on percussion, followed by an improvised percussion duet.

The first AACM groups used multi-instrumentalism extensively in composition, arrangement, and improvisation, particularly the Art Ensemble of Chicago and the Creative Construction Company. "The Light on the Dalta," Smith's composition on the second CCC album, begins with a very short up-tempo theme played on primary instruments that alternates with out-of-time three-way melodic improvising. The instrumental palette expands as the improvising progresses, with Jenkins playing glockenspiel around two minutes in, followed by the introduction of accordion, seal horn, recorder, harmonica, zither, gongs, shakers, and other percussion. Braxton plays solos on flute and clarinet, as well as alto saxophone, and the piece concludes with a free-time unison melody.

"Silence," Smith's piece on the third CCC album, does not have any composed material. It seems instead to be a rule-based improvisation. The musicians alternate individually playing a sound or phrase, leaving silences in-between that are longer than the sounds or phrases. Around four minutes in, Smith plays a phrase consisting of single hits on a triangle, a wood block, and a small gong, concluding with a trumpet growl. Over a minute and a half of silence follows. After a long tone from Braxton on contrabass clarinet and another extended silence, Smith plays trumpet and gongs simultaneously at the seven-minute mark, halfway through the track. This one-man ensemble is followed by the first real ensemble, where gongs, recorder, and zither are briefly heard together. The group moves into more simultaneous and interactive playing in the second half but maintains a connection to the extraordinary restraint of the initial premise.

Smith's "The Bell," recorded by the CCC on Braxton's *Three Compositions of New Jazz*, has a composed theme bracketing solos on the musicians' primary instruments. In one passage of the theme, Smith notated rhythms and dynamics while leaving pitch, tempo, and all other elements up to the performers.[32] Inspired by the results, he began exploring ways of specifying ratios of sound to silence in the interpretation of his themes and in improvisation, an approach he named "rhythm units." Rather than measuring notes and rests in relation to a tempo or in relation to each other, Smith describes each note in proportion to its adjacent silence, formalizing the relationships from the first half of "Silence." This is a new approach to organizing musical time.[33] Smith has expanded this into his own notational system, named "ankhrasmation," combining the Egyptian ankh, "ras" meaning father, and "ma" for mother.[34] He distinguishes ankhrasmation from graphic notation because it is a structure based on freedom rather than freedom based on structure. Instead of allowing improvisation within a composition, it assumes improvisation as the essence of a performance, then composes some parameters for it. He has also described ankhrasmation as a syntax with no words. It can indicate speed, volume, density, and contour, but the specific sounds are up to the players.[35]

Language Music

One of the enduring shocks of Ornette Coleman's music is that his pieces not only worked differently from common practice but from each other, offering a variety of alternatives, what Paul Bley called the "premise" of each composition.[36] Anthony Braxton, Wadada Leo Smith's partner in the Creative Construction Company, is an extremely prolific creator of premises and systems. He has also chosen to explain this work in depth, publishing the three-volume theoretical *Tri-Axium Writings*, five volumes of *Composition Notes*, teaching for decades at Mills College and Wesleyan University, and establishing the Tri-Centric Foundation to preserve, publish, and promote his work.[37] This transparency has facilitated an extensive secondary literature.

Braxton's compositions are titled with a mix of letters, numbers, drawings, and collages, and these graphic titles have been mistaken for graphic scores. While Braxton does use graphic notation, among other formats, the titles are not scores. They represent aspects of the music, but only in the way that a title like "Toccata and Fugue in D Minor" does. Smith has claimed that "any advanced student of mysticism or metaphysical science can readily read the code and symbolism embedded in his titles," while Braxton himself has indicated they encode compositional elements, friends' initials, and chess moves, as well as more esoteric elements.[38] These titles have presented a challenge to discussions of this music, since they are untypable and unpronounceable, so it has become standard to refer to compositions by their numbers rather than their titles. Some groups of related compositions share a number and are lettered, such as Compositions 77A through J, a set of solo material created for the album *Alto Saxophone Improvisations 1979*.

Here are some Braxton compositions and their distinctive premises and techniques:

- Composition 4, originally for five tubas, has no staff lines. Rhythms, articulations, dynamics, and melodic shapes are given, but the specific pitches are up to the players.[39]
- Composition 6C is a circus march on a repeating root-fifth bass line.[40]
- Composition 6F maintains a fixed unison rhythm throughout. The players improvise by using different pitches and sounds to play this unchanging rhythm.[41]
- Composition 10, originally for solo piano, is a set of sixty-eight graphics on nine pages that can be played in any order and for any durations.[42]
- Composition 18 is a string quartet using graphic notation for pitch. There are no rhythms, but the total duration of each line of music is given. The performers can decide to play the three sections in any order or combination, to play the phrases within a section in any order, and to play each phrase forward or backward.[43]
- Composition 23C is a cumulative form. The musicians play bar 1, then bars 1 and 2, then 1, 2, and 3, until the full line is played, then they subtract bars in the same order, playing bar 2 to the end, then bar 3 to the end, 4 to the end, and so on.[44] This type of form is found in some folk songs such as "The Twelve Days of Christmas," but it is very rare in jazz or related music. One close relative is "Les Moutons de Panurge," by Frederic Rzewski, which Braxton played when he toured with Rzewski and the other members of Musica Elettronica Viva in 1970.[45] However, unlike Rzewski's piece, where the players are expected to accidentally fall out of synch and directed to not correct themselves if they do, generating an anarchist minimalism, Braxton's is played in unison while the drummer takes a solo.[46]
- Composition 40M is an angular line played over a one note vamp that continues under the solos.
- Composition 58 is a John Philip Sousa tribute, but includes an improvised solo played over an asymmetrical oompah

pattern that creates a skipping record effect and another accompanied by layered nonsynchronized loops and breath noise.[47]

- Composition 59 accompanies the soloists with unison cued hits. As it progresses, more and more players are directed to hold notes or play figures between the hits, creating an increasingly foggy texture.[48]

- Composition 69Q is another cumulative form, but instead of lengthening and shortening the melody, it expands and contracts the improvisational space attached to a repeated four-bar melody: theme, one bar of improvisation, theme, two bars of improvisation, theme, three bars of improvisation, building up to eight bars of improvising and then back down.

- Composition 76 uses color and shapes in the score but leaves their interpretation to the players. Its pages can be played in any order, and each page includes traditionally notated materials to be played together on cue as well as "modular notation," where mixed graphic and standard elements can be used independently by the players, who are also directed to use their voices and multiple instruments.[49] The improvisation sections include codes for the number of notes or phrases to be played, whether instruments or voice should be used, and whether a player should dominate, support, or be neutral.[50]

- Composition 114 is a C major scale, with each player looping fragments of different lengths, creating a texture like early Philip Glass.[51]

- Composition 115 is an angular postbop melody with a second staff showing a rising and falling line indicating increasing and decreasing the tempo, establishing what Braxton calls an "accordion sound space."[52]

There are also many pieces based on the Ornette Coleman model, where a swinging theme frames "time, no changes" solos, and those where a rubato theme brackets improvisations without rhythmic accompaniment, as in the Creative Construction Company. The one structure Braxton seems to have never used is song form: none of his over four hundred compositions has a repeating cycle of chord changes, although he has made numerous recordings of others' compositions in this form.

Braxton has cited Karlheinz Stockhausen as a model of developing a distinct language for each piece.[53] He also has often told a sort of origin story about his first attempt at the solo concert required of AACM members. He had intended to play a marathon spontaneous improvisation following the example of John Coltrane but ran out of ideas and energy much sooner than planned. This inspired him to organize his musical materials so that he could draw on them more economically instead of burning through them all in a few minutes. His categories included types of sounds (long tones, multiphonics, etc.) and ways of combining sounds (smooth or angular lines, wide or small intervals, etc.). By 1988, he had a list of over a hundred available "sound classifications" but focused primarily on a dozen "Language Types":

1. long sound
2. accented long sound
3. trills
4. staccato line formings
5. intervallic formings
6. multiphonics
7. short attacks
8. angular attacks
9. legato formings
10. diatonic formings
11. gradient formings
12. subidentity formings[54]

A simple application of this system is to pick one language type and improvise with it, then select another, or to choose two and explore their combinations and contrasts. This is the basis of most of Braxton's solo saxophone music, which specifies types of material but not the material itself.⁵⁵ For example, Composition 77H consists of these directions:

1. Trills strategies—as a primary ingredient or the basic structure of the music

2. Register decisions—as a basis for establishing areas of investigation

3. Fast to slow trill sections—on a single note

4. Trill tempo variations—inside of a given phrase construction

5. Melodic shape formations—a kind of song-like approach

6. Nothing too forced

7. Trill speed factoring—a. medium fast trill lines, b. combination line formings (of 2 or more trill speeds)

8. Medium to medium/slow general pulse.⁵⁶

It is not an accident that there are twelve Language Types. Like Stockhausen, Braxton is interested in astrology and other esoteric systems, so the parallel to the twelve zodiac signs is deliberate. When Braxton began writing a set of operas in the 1980s, akin to Wagner's *Ring* and Stockhausen's *Licht*, he planned a dozen operas and associated each of the dozen major characters with a Language Type. Likewise, as he organized his musical world into multiple systems in the new millennium, he associated each system with a Language Type.⁵⁷

Braxton's Composition 23G, from 1975, was a pivotal work. It puts a typically jumpy melody over an unpredictable stop-time pattern of bass and drum "sound attacks" that continues under the solos. Braxton developed this idea further in 1984 with Compositions 108A–D, which he called "pulse tracks." They are designed to be played under improvisations or other compositions, usually by the bass and drums, and include melodic figures, sound attacks, and measured spaces for improvisation.⁵⁸ On the 1985 UK quartet tour documented in Graham Lock's book *Forces in Motion*, the sets combined pulse tracks with other compositions, the band had assorted parts from Composition 96 (originally for chamber orchestra) that they could insert, and pianist Marilyn Crispell also had Compositions

1 and 30–33 (originally for piano) to draw from.[59] Recordings from this period onwards often feature track titles such as "Composition 159 (+30 +108A)," representing these layered performances. Braxton increasingly saw his body of work as an environment rather than as discrete pieces. In his 1988 "Introduction to 'Catalogue of Works,'" he stated that "all compositions in my music system connect together" and "all instrumental parts in my group of musics are autonomous."[60]

After moving from the distinct premises of separate pieces to this collage logic in the 1980s, Braxton began developing multiple collage logics in the 1990s, a set of metapremises. The first of these was the Ghost Trance Music, consisting of over one hundred and fifty pieces composed between 1995 and 2006. These endless melodies serve as a route through Braxton's catalog.

Ghost Trance Music comes in four "species." First species Ghost Trance Music is a stream of even notes, played in nontransposed unison (like Ornette Coleman's *Skies of America*) and without rests. After a few minutes, some sections are marked to be looped and some notes have shapes attached, which represent offramps to other musical areas. At a triangle (which for Braxton represents "intuitive realization/synthesis or correspondence logics"), players can leave the melody to play "secondary material"—graphic scores appended to each Ghost Trance piece—at a square ("concrete realization/stable logic"), they can draw from other compositions, and at a circle ("abstract realization/mutable logics"), they can improvise freely or with Language Types. Second species Ghost Trance Music adds dynamics, occasional rhythmic variations, and more frequent shapes and loops. Third species has almost no even notes, adds articulations, uses graphic notation ("imaginary realization") in the primary melody, and does not include loops. Fourth species, "accelerator whip," has no even notes and no shapes or loops but adds color (with an interpretive key).[61] There is also Syntactical Ghost Trance Music, with words and syllables for vocalists.[62]

Braxton called the album *9 Compositions (Iridium) 2006* "THE point of definition in my work so far."[63] It features his 12+1 tet, composed primarily of his former students from Wesleyan University, some of whom are now themselves prominent composer/performers, such as Mary Halvorson and Steve Lehman. This group also reflected Braxton's moves toward gender equity. In addition to Halvorson, it included flutist Nicole Mitchell, violinist/violist Jessica Pavone, trombonist Reut Regev, and bassoonist Sarah Schoenbeck. The players' deep knowledge of his work, plus the extensive liner notes and documentary and performance video included, make it the clearest and most accessible representation of Ghost Trance Music.

The Sonic Genome is Ghost Trance Music on an epic scale, with productions lasting multiple hours and involving dozens of musicians. At the version presented in Vancouver in 2010, performers had a group of Ghost Trance compositions of various species to choose from, so that Ghost Trance Music in general rather than a single piece served as the core. Each member of the 12+1 tet led a squad of players, serving as officers under Braxton's leadership, but musicians were also scheduled to leave their units and assemble to perform certain pieces, and squads merged, dissolved, and reformed over the event. The Vancouver Genome took place in a former train roundhouse, appropriate to Braxton's love of transit metaphors for his music systems, while museums in Berlin and Turin have hosted others. The performers and audience move around these multi-room venues, a physical expression of their navigation through Braxton's oeuvre.[64] By walking among the performers, each listener improvises a mix and edit from the simultaneous ensembles and soloists exploring multiple compositions and types of improvisation.

Ghost Trance Music corresponds to Language Type 1: long sound, because the main themes of Ghost Trance Music are each a continuous line: a single extremely long sound. In Echo Echo Mirror House Music, the players move through improvisations based on the Language Types following graphic scores overlaid with transparencies and signals from a conductor. However, the distinguishing feature of Echo Echo Mirror House Music, and possibly the source of its name, is that each musician triggers recordings of Braxton's music in addition to playing instruments. Echo Echo Mirror House Music seems like a portable way to achieve the multicompositional and multi-ensemble textures of the Sonic Genome, but it is a distinct musical system because it has its own organizational and notational forms and does not have the through-line of Ghost Trance Music. It corresponds to Language Type 6: multiphonics or sound mass.[65] Braxton has also presented Falling River Music, based on Language Type 2: accented long sound, Diamond Curtain Wall Music, based on Type 3: trills or ornamentation, Pine Top Aerial Music, which combines sound and movement, corresponding to Language Type 7: short attacks, and ZIM Music, based on Type 11: gradient formings.[66]

Zooid

In 1969, AACM saxophonist Henry Threadgill played alongside Wadada Leo Smith on Muhal Richard Abrams's album *Young at Heart/Wise in Time*, then didn't record again until the debut of his trio Air in 1975. With Air and his subsequent Sextett, Threadgill ranged from reinterpretations of rags by Scott Joplin and Jelly Roll Morton to free improvisation but focused on his original work. Both bands were critically and commercially successful, and Threadgill was acclaimed as a composer with a unique and ingenious take on the entire history of jazz. For example, "Spotted Dick Is Pudding" from the Sextett's 1987 album *Easily Slip into Another World* is essentially an eight-bar melody that Louis Armstrong might have played. Threadgill plays it twice on alto saxophone, then it is played twice by trumpet and twice by trombone. Each of the six renditions is phrased and embellished differently, and it modulates symmetrically by using an augmented chord instead of a dominant seventh at the end of every other chorus. Because all the intervals in an augmented chord are the same, any of its notes can be the root. The alto statement is in the key of A, the trumpet a major third lower in F, and the trombone a major third lower in D-flat. Moving down another major third from D-flat returns the band to A for the alto saxophone solo, followed by solos by the other horns, each in the key in which they played the melody.

Threadgill is also interested in unusual instrumentation. While Air was a saxophone, bass, and drums trio, the Sextett added trumpet, trombone, cello, and another drummer. He counted the two drummers as a single unit, yielding a seven-member sextet, possibly represented by the extra "t" which makes "sextet" a seven-letter word. X-75 was four flutes, four basses, and voice, and Very Very Circus was saxophone, trombone or French horn, two guitars, two tubas, and drums. Zooid, his main band since 2001, has consisted of saxophone, guitar, trombone doubling on tuba, drums, and cello, oud, or electric bass.

Before Zooid, Threadgill was stretching harmony and counterpoint, finding new ways to write and play within common practice. On Zooid's second album, 2009's *This Brings Us to Volume 1*, he introduced an original system for organizing pitches, setting aside the major/minor and chord/scale relationships central to Western music.[67]

In the major/minor system, a triad is built from the first, third, and fifth notes of a scale, and that scale is the gravitational center for melodies composed or improvised over that chord. The Zooid system focuses on the intervals between the notes rather than the specific notes. Threadgill begins with a set of three notes and generates what he calls its "sister cells" by inverting the intervals that each note participates in. There are three notes, and each note has two intervals, its relationships to the other two. Each of these six intervals is inverted, producing six sisters. For example, in the set C E G, the E is a minor third below the G, so it moves to a minor third above, producing C G B-flat. The G is a minor third above the E, so it flips to a minor third below, yielding C C-sharp E, and so on. The descendants of C E G are: C G B-flat, C C-sharp E, E A-flat G, A C G, E G D, and F C E.

The intervals in the family of cells define the available melodic material, much as a chord in the major/minor system defines its melodic material through its affiliated scale. The six sisters of C E G include a minor second, minor third, major third, fifth, minor seventh, and major seventh. Threadgill represents this as -2, -3, 3, 5, -7, 7. However, this is not relative to the tonic; he does not simply use the invented scale C D-flat E-flat E G B-flat B over a C triad. Rather, the soloists may use any pitches, but only the given intervals. Even though the invented scale includes D-flat and G, a soloist could not play D-flat to G, because that is a flatted fifth and that interval is not in the set, but they could play A-flat to A, even though neither is in the invented scale, because A-flat to A is a minor second, and that is a permitted interval.[68] Instead of chord changes Threadgill's scores give improvisers the original cell, the number of beats it lasts, and the available intervals.[69]

This system has some connection to Ornette Coleman's harmolodics, John Coltrane's work, particularly from *A Love Supreme* on, and Cecil Taylor's unit structures, all of which use transposition of intervals and melodic shapes as a unifying principle in place of vertical harmony. It is also inspired by Elliott Carter's use of set theory in his post-serial compositions, and by Muhal Richard Abrams's AACM pedagogy. Abrams taught chords and scales primarily as groups of intervals, counting by half steps to call a major scale two 2, 2, 1 groups connected by a 2, for example.[70]

The Zooid system presented a substantial challenge to Threadgill's band. Guitarist Liberty Ellman said it took him four or five years to feel comfortable improvising in the system. While he could play solos by ear that sounded good, he hadn't assimilated the language.[71] His ear and his sense of what sounded good were grounded in music based on other systems. None of the musical vocabulary or finger habits he had acquired playing jazz, rock, R and B, and other musics applied. Ellman eventually arrived at an approach analogous to chord/scale playing: he targets the notes of each cell and links them with lines constructed from combinations of the permitted intervals.[72]

Threadgill's use of meter is also unorthodox. He composes without bar lines, then adds them based on the length of the melodic phrases, rather than starting with a form or groove and putting the melody over it. This results in constantly changing meter.[73] He also encourages his drummers to divide phrases differently from the rest of the band. For example, a thirty-one-beat melodic phrase might be grouped 7, 7, 5, 3, 3, 6 for the pitched instruments but played by the drummer as 7, 7, 7, 7, 3. Everyone's part audibly fits together, but because downbeats land asymmetrically and unpredictably, it is challenging to hear exactly how this coordination is achieved.[74] As with the pitch system, it is obvious that this music is highly organized, but in complex and unfamiliar ways.

Threadgill's compositions are dramatically rearranged for each performance during extensive rehearsals. In his thesis on Zooid, Chad Taylor analyzes the performance of "See the Blackbird Now" on the album *Tomorrow Sunny/The Revelry, Spp*. It opens with a cello improvisation over two measures from the middle of the melody looped in what Threadgill calls "long meter," where each cell lasts twice as many beats as during the theme, then the first five measures of the melody are played as written, followed by a bass flute solo over an eight-bar long meter loop, then another segment of the melody as written, and so on. There are further solos over loops, some of which use sections of the composed material played backwards, as well as more bits of the melody, free improvisations, and unaccompanied solos. The original written music is never played straight through.[75] Younger musicians including Tyshawn Sorey, Matt Mitchell, and Kate Gentile have adopted similarly elastic approaches to their compositions, choosing different elements to loop, prolong, use cumulatively, invert, or reverse in each performance.[76]

Conduction

In 1985, Lawrence "Butch" Morris recorded *Current Trends in Racism in Modern America: A Work in Progress*, the first document of the system for directing improvisers he called "Conduction." At the same time that Morris was establishing himself as a cornetist and as a composer of memorable melodies for David Murray's groups, such as "Joanne's Green Satin Dress,"

"Red Car," and "Spoonin'," he began developing a set of hand and baton cues to generate and shape performances as they happened. Morris was not the first to conduct improvisers and regularly acknowledged those who had used the technique before him, from Leonard Bernstein to Frank Zappa. In particular, Sun Ra seems to have created several of his major 1960s albums through conducted improvisation. *The Magic City*, the three volumes of *The Heliocentric Worlds of Sun Ra*, and *Cosmic Tones for Mental Therapy* have no audibly composed material except for the bass line on "Moon Dance" from *Cosmic Tones*, but the ensemble organization suggests Ra was cueing entrances and exits, soloists and accompanists, and possibly giving other signals.[77] However, Morris was the first to make conducted improvisation the center of his creative practice.

Conducting and cueing systems are used either to improvise arrangements or to arrange improvisations. Morris began with the former, from an interest in spontaneously reshaping written music. What if the conductor could change the order of sections of a piece or their expressive characteristics during the performance? Morris encountered this approach in the mid-1970s when he played in Horace Tapscott's Pan-Afrikan People's Arkestra, then applied it when he led David Murray's big band in 1984, as documented on *Live at Sweet Basil*, volumes 1 and 2.[78] That year he also created a concert from a Beethoven string quartet movement by selecting five sections of the original piece that could be cued at any time and by using hand signs to direct the players to repeat, sustain, or improvise.[79]

At the same time that Morris looked at Beethoven and big band scores and imagined spontaneously rearranging them, he also played in free improvisation sessions and thought about similarly shaping those unruly expressions. He believed traditionally notated and structured music didn't challenge improvisers or make good use of their unique abilities, but he also believed that music benefited from central organization; he was not interested in anarchy.[80]

Morris moved from improvising arrangements to arranging improvisation in 1985, performing a conducted improvisation without a score, using only his cues, that was released as *Current Trends in Racism in Modern America* and designated Conduction #1. He subsequently reserved the term "Conduction" for pieces without composed material, referring to later performances based on scores as "Induction."[81]

Conduction is content neutral. The players improvise the material and the conductor arranges it.[82] This enabled Morris to combine musicians from multiple traditions, instruments in multiple tuning systems, electronics, spoken word, and so on. Although he worked with dozens of virtuoso instrumentalists, anyone who could produce some kind of controlled sound and follow cues could perform in a Conduction.

For *Current Trends in Racism in Modern America*, Morris used the repeat, sustain, and improvise signs from his Beethoven Induction and added gestures to adjust volume and to trigger full-group improvisation. Over the next twenty-five years and two hundred Conductions, he ended up with a vocabulary of around sixty signs.[83] However, these are mostly variations of a much smaller core group. The simpler the cueing language, the more quickly players can decode it and respond.

One of Morris's most original signs is the memory cue. The conductor points to their temple with one hand, holds up a number of fingers with the other, then indicates starting and ending points with baton downbeats. Whatever is played between those beats is stored as that numbered memory and can be recalled at any time. Half an hour later, the conductor might cue that memory and the musicians will be expected to immediately return to the stored material, like a tape loop or sampler.[84] This enables the conductor to move, repeat, juxtapose, and layer improvised elements in a real-time composition or remix.

Walter Thompson's Soundpainting system is an interesting contrast to Conduction. While Morris only created new signs if they did something that could not be done in notation and tried to focus Conduction on sounds and forms that could not be created in either scored or improvised music, Soundpainting gives many options to indicate more traditionally defined content. It includes over 750 signs, used in the syntax "who, what, how, and when." A cue could say, "These three people will play in B-flat major, fast detached notes, on the next downbeat," but not all elements of the syntax are in every cue; a conductor can choose how much to leave up to the players. There are also "mode" and "palette" signs to designate specific vocabulary and material respectively, allowing a conductor to call for idiomatic playing or work with a composition.[85]

Composer/percussionist Adam Rudolph provides original melodic, harmonic, and rhythmic material to his ensembles and uses a small group of cues to spontaneously organize it. Some of his pieces, such as "Dance Drama," are performed using a consistent sequence and could be rewritten as linear compositions, while "Walking the Curve" is a pentatonic vamp played under solos, usually used as a finale or encore. He also gives some members of the group conventionally notated pieces that he may cue as interludes or layer with other material.

However, most of Rudolph's work draws on a set of modules that are spontaneously combined from performance to performance. These include "pitch matrices," grids of note names that he cues the group through vertically or horizontally in unison or parallel, or signals as the basis of improvisations; "pictograms," notes from Yusef Lateef's triple-diminished scale arranged to form vines, leaves, flowers, or mandalas; and "ostinatos of circularity," repeated riffs based on his deep study of African, Indian, Arabic, and other rhythmic systems and on his concept of "cyclic verticalism."

Cyclic verticalism creates long, complex, and exciting rhythms by superimposing shorter ones: a five beat pattern and a seven beat one will land on a common downbeat every thirty-five beats, for example.[86] Musicians customarily break meters longer than three beats into groups of twos and threes, so five will be either 3-2 or 2-3 and seven 3-2-2, 2-2-3, or 2-3-2, so a rhythmic overlay such as five and seven won't just produce accents every fifth and seventh beat but also a generate a lattice of threes and twos, as this diagram of 3-2 over 3-2-2 shows:

```
X..X.X..X.X..X.X..X.X..X.X..X.X..X.
X..X.X.X..X.X.X..X.X.X..X.X.X..X.X.
```

Rudolph further unpacks this concept and diagrams some of his favorite metric combinations in his book *Pure Rhythm*.[87]

Conducted improvisation creates a clear power relationship: the players are required to focus their attention on the conductor and instantly obey directions. Yielding control of major elements of their performance challenges some players' sense of individuality and freedom. If they wanted someone to tell them what, when, and how to play, they would have become classical or pop musicians, not improvisers. Also, authorship can become problematic when material improvised by a group is shaped into a work signed and owned by the conductor.[88] Several members of the ensemble assembled for Morris's 1997 British tour mutinied and quit rather than submit to his authority and aesthetic. Some who stayed subsequently formed the London Improvisers Orchestra to continue exploring conducted improvisation in a more egalitarian and polyglot format.[89]

John Zorn played alto saxophone on *Current Trends in Racism in Modern America* in February 1985. That October, he first documented his game piece "Cobra." Zorn has since recorded hundreds of albums featuring everything from noise to easy listening, but his first recognition as a composer came from a series of pieces inspired by various sports and games. Like Conduction, Zorn's game pieces have no material, only relationships, and are idiom and technique neutral.[90] As he explained, "What I was really fascinated with was finding a way to harness these improvisors' talents in a compositional framework without actually hindering what they did best." For example, "Archery" is simply a sequence of all the possible subgroupings of a twelve-member band. What each subgroup plays is improvised by the musicians. Subsequent game pieces became less linear, culminating in "Cobra."[91]

"Cobra" complicates the relationship between the players and the conductor, who Zorn calls a "prompter." Unlike the conductors in other systems, the prompter does not originate cues. Instead, the players use a combination of cards and hand signs to propose cues to the prompter, who selects which of them to relay to the ensemble to perform. Players also have the option to go rogue and ignore cues by donning a headband and can form "guerrilla units" to work outside the system.[92]

Anthony Braxton used a simple set of gestures to conduct his big band in "Language Improvisations" on their 1978 European tour by cuing the use of various Language Types and employed multiple simultaneous conductors on projects including *4 Compositions (Ulrichsberg) 2005 Phonomanie VIII* and the Sonic Genome. In his 12+1 tet any member could spontaneously form a subensemble and lead it into part of the primary Ghost Trance composition, its secondary material, another composition, or Language Music, using hand signs, whispers, and directions written on small whiteboards, as documented on *9 Compositions (Iridium) 2006*.

Bassist/composer William Parker has similarly decentered the leadership of his Little Huey Creative Orchestra. The group contains seven "stations": trombones, trumpets, baritone sax and tuba, soprano and tenor saxophones, alto saxophones, drums, and basses. Each has its own leader, who can cue composed material or generate new ideas in performance, and the players can also function individually. Parker does not usually conduct but provides some themes and gives occasional cues using hand signs or colored pieces of paper.[93] He has essentially implemented a free jazz version of the early big band approach of "head arrangements" and "setting riffs," where groups would improvise on a standard chord progression with section leaders coordinating backing figures. The most successful of these combinations of riffs, such as Count

Basie's "Jumpin' at the Woodside," would be committed to memory as "head arrangements," named, and later fixed as compositions through recordings and sheet music.

Since forming in 1977, the Bay Area ROVA Saxophone Quartet (originally Jon Raskin, Larry Ochs, Andrew Voight, and Bruce Ackley; Voight has been replaced by Steve Adams) has worked extensively with cueing systems and games, including in collaborations with John Zorn, Anthony Braxton, and Butch Morris. "Radar" is their name for an overall system encompassing multiple sets of cues for sound-types and processes including some adapted from Zorn and Morris such as the "memory" cue. In various pieces and at various stages of their work, the games and signaling languages included in Radar might be used in a planned sequence or spontaneously instigated by the players and could include composed material or not. They include relatively basic forms, such as solo, duo, or trio subgroup improvisations or a collective drone, as well as some rather complex ones.

As in Zorn's game pieces, issues of freedom and control within the ensemble are often in play. For example, the "cage" game, drawn from a piece by Adams, consists of ten cues, which any player can give to any other:

1. Do something else.

2. Stop.

3. Play outside outside.

4. Play inside inside.

5. Play behind.

6. Play in front.

7. Halve what you are doing.

8. Fill the silences.

9. Play with only one pitch, two pitches or three pitches (as cued).

10. Join a specific person (as cued) in what he is doing.

Players may not drop out or change their playing on their own. In contrast, the "fierce story" game divides the group into two duos. Player one solos expressively, telling a "fierce story," supported by player two. They continue until player three decides to enters with a fierce story, with or without the support of player four, and the two solos or duos continue interrupting each other for the duration of the game. In "cage," each player has power over everyone except themselves, while in "fierce story" players one and three each choose when to replace the other in the spotlight and whether to do it alone or with their duo partner.[94]

Search and Reflect

Trombonist Paul Rutherford, drummer John Stevens, and saxophonist Trevor Watts began performing as the core of the Spontaneous Music Ensemble at the Little Theatre Club in London in January 1966.[95] On the SME's debut album, *Challenge*, recorded that March, their interest in the first wave of American free jazz was clear from the first two tracks: "E.D.'s Message," for Eric Dolphy, and "2.B. Ornette." By their second album, *Karyobin*, recorded in 1968 with Kenny Wheeler, Evan Parker, Derek Bailey, and Dave Holland, Stevens had asserted himself as the group's leader and only consistent member. He also had discarded the composed themes and "time, no changes" approach of *Challenge* for collective improvisation based on an austere set of guidelines, explaining:

> My intention was to break up the line as it went on; concentrate itself more and more, and break it into smaller and smaller pieces, so that we ended up playing in a very detailed fashion, in the same way that a pointillist painter would choose to use dots.
>
> I was working towards a non-linear way of playing. I was trying to attract the group toward that by relating to the moment in order to hear all the instruments within the musical environment, rather than develop the improvisation in a linear way—meaning that the individual didn't develop individual lines.[96]

Evan Parker similarly said:

> There was a lot of talk about, how can we get to the real *group* free music? And it did seem to be about the fragmentation of any one particular contribution, so you could see it had parallels

with Webern and *Klangfarbenmelodie*—that notion of the total group statement not being derivable from superimposed linearities but from pointillistic atomized contributions. So, if you analyze any one of the players, you don't hear a coherent line; it's only by putting the whole thing together that you hear a coherent group music.[97]

Klangfarbenmelodie, which translates to "sound-color melody," is the compositional technique of dividing a melodic line between instruments. As Parker described, it treats the ensemble as a unit rather than a collection of individuals. It also allows the sequence of sound-colors itself to become a structural element, so a pattern like "flute, violin, trumpet" can function like a melody or a rhythm, able to be repeated, varied, extended, and so on.

The players on *Karyobin* improvise klangfarbenmelodie by playing short phrases and attempting to start when someone else stops, creating a sense of lines moving through the group. Because the trumpet, saxophone, guitar, bass, and drums lineup resembles a jazz quintet, it is often possible to hear what is happening as a solo and a rhythm section, call and response, or brief solo breaks, even though all five members are equally active and lines pass between them evenly.

After an experience with audience participation during a 1968 SME performance at the Little Theatre Club, Stevens began creating text instructions that would be accessible to nonmusicians but also interesting for musicians.[98] These were used in workshops and performances for much of the 1970s and published in the book *Search and Reflect*.[99] Stevens started the Community Music movement in 1983, using *Search and Reflect* to teach fundamental musicianship to students of all levels across all styles of music, and it has endured as part of British music education far beyond the worlds of free jazz or experimental music.[100]

Stevens's first workshop piece, "Familie," was based on deep breathing, offering a series of pitches, each to be played as long as possible in a single breath.[101] His next works, "Click Piece" and "Sustained Piece," set aside even that level of traditional musical content, calling simply for the players to produce the shortest and most consistent sounds possible ("clicks") or to hold a sound for the length of their exhalation ("sustain").[102] These workshop pieces run parallel to the text scores of Pauline Oliveros, Karlheinz Stockhausen, and artists connected to Fluxus including John

Cage, Yoko Ono, LaMonte Young, and Naim June Paik.[103] However, many of those are closer to aphorisms, poems, koans, or prompts for meditation such as Ono's "Water Piece," which consists simply of the word "Water," or unperformable conceptual works, such as Paik's "Danger Music No. 5," which asks the performer to enter a whale's birth canal.[104] In contrast, Stevens's texts are always practical, designed for pedagogy and performance.

Between *Challenge* and *Karyobin*, Stevens developed a drum set specifically for the SME, using smaller, higher-pitched, and less resonant drums and cymbals for clearer articulation and to leave more space for the other musicians to be heard. His focus on clicks and sustains as the essential elements of SME music connected the group to his evolving drum language.[105] It also demanded similar restraint from his collaborators. While Stevens admired the heroic individualism of John Coltrane and Albert Ayler, he believed the time for that sort of playing had passed. This was a significant challenge to musicians like Derek Bailey, Evan Parker, and Trevor Watts, who were not always willing to sublimate their personal voices for the discipline of the SME.[106] As Stevens enforced his concepts on the SME, Trevor Watts started his own band, Amalgam, using players from the same community, sometimes including Stevens, in order to continue playing music that included themes, grooves, and solos.[107] Likewise, Stevens himself also sometimes led groups using some more conventional elements and performed non-SME free improvisations with Bailey, Parker, and others.

Stevens described the SME as "one of the closest examples human beings can get to nature," "being in tune, as close as possible, with all the people that are around you, and at the same time contributing." The instructions in *Search and Reflect* often focus more on what to listen for than what to play. Stevens claimed the music would "take care of itself," that the discipline of improvisation was about listening to the rest of the ensemble rather than thinking about one's own performance or the outcome: "Nothing you had to say was more important than an awareness of the whole."[108] The depth of listening and interaction is what makes performances succeed, not the material played.[109]

Evan Parker questioned this goal of egoless playing, arguing that some assertion of will is required to start and steer an improvisation and that the essential challenge as an improviser is not to disappear into a group but to find how to be yourself in one.[110] He reframed Stevens's core ideas as follows:

(1) If you can't hear somebody else you are playing too loud, and (2) if what you are doing does not, at regular intervals, make reference to what you are hearing other people do, you might as well not be playing in the group.[111]

Most of the pieces in *Search and Reflect* offer a series of increasingly challenging or open variations, usually concluding with the possibility of moving into unstructured free improvisation. "Click Piece" and "Sustained Piece" follow this model, which typified SME performances from approximately 1968 to 1973. The album *Face to Face*, from 1973, is an especially dramatic example. It consists of multiple versions of the title piece played by Stevens and Trevor Watts. The text directs each musician to play for the benefit of the other, to pay as little attention as possible to playing and to try "to be a total ear to the other player." When each feels this has been achieved, they can proceed to more conversational improvising.[112] As Stevens put it:

Free group improvisation is our aim, and a preparation piece like this is to aid us to achieve the concentration required for the best results. The actual process, loosely described in these notes, may only take a few seconds, but those few seconds are significant in getting us beyond ourselves and into the music.[113]

The SME mostly improvised without Stevens's texts after 1975, but by then his ideas had spread through his book, workshops, and recordings, making formal "preparation pieces" unnecessary.

5

Self-determination

For some artists and commentators, freeing jazz from song form represented freedom from the constraints of the commercial music business. Jazz artists had improvised on pop material at least since the first jazz recordings, such as the Original Dixieland Jazz Band's 1917 version of the Tin Pan Alley hit "(Back Home in) Indiana," and jazz grew alongside American popular song and musical theater. Many beloved works, such as Coleman Hawkins's "Body and Soul," Dizzy Gillespie's "I Can't Get Started," Charlie Parker's "Embraceable You" and *Bird with Strings*, Miles Davis's "My Funny Valentine" and *Porgy and Bess*, and Ella Fitzgerald's series of songbook albums devoted to composers such as Cole Porter, Richard Rogers, and George Gershwin, are interpretations of popular songs. Original melodies written over the chord progressions of songs by Gershwin, Porter, and their peers account for another major segment of the jazz repertoire and canon, and until the late 1950s jazz composers' original work almost always used harmonic and structural models from the American songbook. Improvisers developed their musical languages to creatively navigate these forms.

However, for Amiri Baraka in the 1960s, Black musicians turning from popular songs and related song forms to free improvisation and original musical systems was a rejection of white supremacy. In multiple texts, he described John Coltrane and Sonny Rollins testing the boundaries of song form from the inside, creating space for a new music by exhausting the old. Baraka called them "this new generation's private assassins—demonstrating, perhaps, the final beauties to be extracted from purely chordal jazz." He heard Coltrane attempting to "completely destroy the popular song" on *"Live" at the Village Vanguard* to "prepare an area for [Cecil] Taylor and [Ornette] Coleman" and interpreted Sonny Rollins's 1962 collaborations with Don Cherry as a similar assault on the American songbook from within, writing, "The chief assassin might yet prove to be Sonny Rollins, who had developed a 'perfect' music, and has now—at least in performance, abandoned it in favor of a beautiful efficient 'nihilism.'" Meanwhile, by playing without those structures, "Taylor and Coleman are proceeding as if Coltrane's work had been completed long ago," moving "to restore to jazz its valid separation from, and anarchic disregard of, Western popular forms."[1] In Baraka's dialectical theory of history, a new style emerges from a crisis in an established one. By 1966, he was calling for jazz to abandon Broadway and Tin Pan Alley materials and models entirely, writing, "The new music begins by being free. That is, freed of the popular song. Freed of white American droop, tinkle, etc. The strait jacket of American expression *sans* blackness."[2]

The Jazz Composers Guild

Trumpeter Bill Dixon similarly described free jazz as a move to creative autonomy and self-determination, arguing that African-American creative music should not rely on the forms or materials of the white culture industry:

> With the emergence of the new music, the idea, for the first time of all original music (everything in it being original: the lines or melodies, the harmonies/ when they were overtly present in the forms of chords, etc./) was present in what had previously been called jazz music. There was no grafting onto established harmonies of so-called standards or blues progressions—new lines. That was now passé. As a result, there was no reason for there to be any established anything.[3]

Challenging "any established anything" included questioning how jazz had been presented and recorded. While Baraka's analysis became increasingly Black nationalist and revolutionary during the 1960s, Dixon and Cecil Taylor founded the Jazz Composers Guild in 1964 specifically to advance the new musicians as artists and workers. The members of the Guild—Dixon, Taylor, Carla Bley, Paul Bley, Burton Greene, Michael Mantler, Sun Ra, Roswell Rudd, Archie Shepp, and John Tchicai—represented a wide range of musical approaches and worldviews. They were also exactly half Black and half white.

The Guild developed from a series of performances Dixon produced in New York cafés, art and dance studios, and lofts, focusing on musicians who could not get booked in jazz clubs because they were unknown and their work was outside the mainstream.[4] These led to the 1964 October Revolution in Jazz, the first free jazz festival, and its success inspired him to form an organization. Trained as a painter, Dixon saw his use of alternative venues as parallel to visual artists' opening their studios directly to the public to exhibit and sell work galleries ignored.[5] His plan was that, once the new music achieved recognition through underground shows, commercial venues and labels would be interested, and then the Guild could negotiate on behalf of its members, reforming the jazz business to prevent financial rip-offs and artistic sell-outs.[6] As he put it:

> In this music the power that we have has never been able to be used. And that was the power to withdraw the music from the market, which is what the October Revolution and the Jazz Composers Guild was about. Withdraw the music. In other words, have the situation so that no one would record unless under the auspices where we controlled everything. In that instance we should buy equipment or rent it and record ourselves. The music should only be performed on our territory.[7]

The new music required its own territory in part because it did not conform to the structure or aesthetics of existing jazz clubs, which were bars as well as performance spaces. A. B. Spellman wrote in the liner notes to *Ascension* that it was not meant to be "background music for polite dinner conversation," and he, bassist Buell Neidlinger, and others observed that Cecil Taylor's music was especially ill-suited to barroom settings.[8] In one dramatic incident, Taylor's first attempt to present his mature music in a Black neighborhood jazz club, at the Blue Coronet in Brooklyn in 1962, was brought to an unexpected and violent end by the club's management.[9] On the other end of the dynamic range, Wadada Leo Smith remembers that the Creative Construction Company never played clubs. The silences and small sounds in their music were as inappropriate as the density of Taylor or *Ascension*.[10]

In a 1966 forum, Taylor and Archie Shepp criticized nightclubs as a racialized system of economic exploitation. They also objected to creative limitations imposed by venues, mentioning a recent show where John Coltrane was given thirty-five minutes on a triple bill with singer Carmen McRae and comedian Dick Gregory. They noted his quartet alone could have easily played an hour and a half, and that he had invited several guest horn players that evening who also deserved solo time. Because Taylor and Shepp saw the music in general and Coltrane in particular as high art, they argued presenters needed to adapt to his vision, not the reverse.[11]

When Dixon and Taylor formed the Guild in late 1964, they chose to not invite artists who they considered already established, including Albert Ayler, Don Cherry, and Steve Lacy.[12] They asked Ornette Coleman and John Coltrane to join a proposed strike against jazz clubs, but neither supported the idea and Dixon dropped it, noting that club owners "didn't want avant-garde players in the places anyway."[13] The Guild briefly succeeded in creating alternative performance opportunities, presenting member groups including Sun Ra's Arkestra, Cecil Taylor's Unit, the New York Art Quartet (led by John Tchicai and Roswell Rudd), the Free Form Improvisation Ensemble (led by Burton Greene), Carla Bley and Michael Mantler's Guild Orchestra, and varying ensembles organized by Shepp, Paul Bley, and Dixon himself, multiple times in cafés and lofts.[14] These shows earned major press coverage in *Downbeat*, the *Nation*, the *New Yorker*, and the *New York Times*, but this did not lead to offers of further work on terms acceptable to the Guild.[15]

Labels approached free jazz with caution. Blue Note released boundary-pushing records by a roster of musicians who had proved themselves in mainstream settings, such as Herbie Hancock, Andrew Hill, Freddie Hubbard, Bobby Hutcherson, Jackie McLean, Grachan Moncur III, Sam Rivers, Wayne Shorter, Tony Williams, and Larry Young, but avoided unknown and untested musicians. They released Eric Dolphy's *Out to Lunch* after he had led several albums on Prestige and been featured with John Coltrane, Ornette Coleman, Oliver Nelson, Max Roach, Abbey Lincoln, and Charles Mingus, signed Don Cherry after he left Coleman's quartet, and began working with Coleman himself in 1965, after his historic series of Atlantic recordings. Cecil Taylor recorded *Unit Structures* and *Conquistador* for Blue Note in 1966, after his work with the Guild had raised his profile.

Blue Note considered a free jazz release successful if it broke even.[16] Label owners Alfred Lion and Frances Wolff were interested in the new music but had no illusions about its commercial appeal. Not every project had to be a hit, but they could not afford too many that lost money. Apart from Taylor, no Guild members recorded for Blue Note.

Ashley Kahn entitled his book on Impulse Records *The House that Trane Built*, which especially describes their connection to the avant-garde. John Coltrane was their flagship artist, the members of his classic quartet and Alice Coltrane and Pharoah Sanders from his final group all led Impulse sessions, and most of the free jazz players Impulse recorded in the 1960s came through his recommendation, such as Archie Shepp, Marion Brown, and Albert Ayler.[17] The label and artists emphasized this lineage. Shepp's Impulse debut, *Four for Trane*, featured four Coltrane compositions and one of his own, and Marion Brown followed suit with *Three for Shepp*, presenting three of his own pieces on the A side and three by his frequent employer Shepp on the B side. Each posed with his sponsor on the album cover. Ayler's 1967 Impulse debut, *Live in Greenwich Village*, opened with a track entitled "For John Coltrane" and, interviewed for the liner notes to his follow-up, *Love Cry*, he proposed a Trinity of free jazz tenor saxophone: John Coltrane "was the Father, Pharoah was the Son, and I was the Holy Ghost."

Bernard Stollman started the ESP-Disk label in 1963 to release an album promoting Esperanto, a proposed universal language. After hearing Albert Ayler, Stollman asked him to record. Ayler, Gary Peacock, and Sunny Murray recorded *Spiritual Unity* in July 1964, and Stollman began exploring the New York jazz underground. He attended the October Revolution and invited every performer to record.[18] ESP released its initial dozen free jazz albums in September 1965: new work by Ayler, Byron Allen, Ran Blake, Paul Bley, Lowell Davidson, Milford Graves, Bob James, Giuseppi Logan, the New York Art Quartet, Sun Ra, and Pharoah Sanders, plus a recording of a 1962 concert by Ornette Coleman. This framed the large group of mostly new performers as Coleman's disciples and heirs and established ESP as a key part of the free jazz art world.[19] Stollman gave the artists complete control and welcomed obscure and eccentric musicians who would have otherwise been unrecorded. However, he was a lightning rod for criticism, for three related reasons.

First, he was a white Jewish businessman producing recordings from a primarily Black scene that was increasingly interested in cultural and economic self-determination. Amiri Baraka questioned who was profiting from ESP in his review of some of its first releases, and calls for Black control of the music grew over the 1960s.[20]

Second, ESP undermined the Jazz Composers Guild's self-produced shows and recording boycott. Stollman organized showcases for ESP artists that sometimes conflicted with Guild events and a number of Guild artists broke ranks to play on those bills.[21] Likewise, some Guild members had recorded for ESP before the Guild set its rules, such as Paul Bley, or waited until after the Guild folded, such as Burton Greene, but others ignored the rules, including Sun Ra. The Guild's attempt to negotiate the conditions of recording and performance for the new music depended on controlling the supply of the music, but ESP and Impulse Records assembled their own rosters of non-Guild free jazz musicians and tempted the Guild's members to defy its constraints.

Although Archie Shepp had recorded *Four for Trane* for Impulse in August 1964, months before the Guild formed, Dixon held him primarily responsible for the failure of the recording boycott.[22] Shepp had been fired from teaching and social work jobs for his radical politics and was working in a department store in 1965.[23] He was married, had four children, and was unwilling to make further financial sacrifices for Dixon's quixotic project. This conflict led to Dixon quitting the Guild and the organization collapsing in spring 1965. As Dixon put it:

> The reason we didn't win was that no one was really 100% committed to a struggle. They were more committed to making the bread. Everyone would tell you, "Man, I've got a wife and kids . . ." What made them think that their family situation was more important than somebody else's?[24]

Finally, Stollman could not dispel the belief that he was exploiting his artists. He claimed ESP offered better terms than other labels and published his standard contract alongside an explanatory interview in the short-lived magazine *Sounds and Fury*, but some artists held lifelong grudges.[25] Looking back, he said, "No one imagined that it would be commercially viable" but also reflected that musicians "assumed they would derive income from their records," concluding, "They were naive and I was as well."[26]

It was very rare for any jazz album to sell more than five thousand copies in the early 1960s.[27] Most ESP releases sold five hundred to one thousand copies, less than half of what it would have taken to earn artist royalties beyond the original advance, and some ESP artists took additional advances against future royalties in order to survive.[28] While Blue Note had hits like Lee Morgan's "The Sidewinder" and Impulse had John Coltrane, ESP had no popular releases to support the less commercial ones. Every title was a terrible risk. Rather than profiting from exploiting radical Black art, Stollman spent approximately $100,000 of his parents' money subsidizing his label before giving up in 1974.[29]

Self-Reliance Productions

Many free jazz recordings were made for established labels such as Blue Note, Impulse, Atlantic, Savoy, Prestige, Arista, and Columbia, or specialized independents such as ESP-Disk, BYG, Black Saint/Soul Note, hatHut, Leo, Emanem, India Navigation, Nessa, Not Two, Eremite, Relative Pitch, Astral Spirits, Pi, Clean Feed, No Business, CIMP, Moers, Victo, and Rogueart, run by fans-turned-patrons like Bernard Stollman. In the late 1960s, artist-owned labels became an important third category. While Dizzy Gillespie, Stan Kenton, Charles Mingus, Max Roach, and others had attempted to start their own labels, Sun Ra was the first free jazz musician to create his own. He and Alton Abraham launched El Saturn Research in 1956 because, as Ra said, "I didn't want to go through all the starving in the attic and all that foolishness. . . . I wanted to bypass that particular trauma they put on artists today."[30] However, since Saturn was a home-based business producing small batches of LPs that were sold almost entirely at concerts and by mail order, it was not much of a barrier to starvation.[31] The "trauma" it bypassed was the loss of creative control. Ra and Abraham were able to determine every element of the music and its presentation.

Drummer Milford Graves was not invited to join the Jazz Composers Guild, because he was not a composer or bandleader, but he performed in several Guild ensembles and appeared on five of the first batch of ESP releases: *The Lowell Davidson Trio*, Paul Bley's *Barrage*, *The New York Art Quartet*, *The Giuseppi Logan Quartet*, and his own *Percussion Ensemble*.[32] Graves and Don Pullen, the pianist from Logan's band, performed at Yale in April 1966. Inspired by Sun Ra, they used their fee from the concert to issue an LP of part of the performance, entitled *Live at Yale University*, on their own label: Self-Reliance Productions (SRP). Like

Ra, they controlled all aspects of the process. They ordered the first pressing of 1,000 copies in plain black sleeves, because that was the least expensive option, then hand-painted them, making each unique. Saturn releases similarly often featured hand-tinted or otherwise customized covers. SRP also followed Saturn in controlling their own distribution, selling primarily at shows and by mail order. Amiri Baraka helped drive sales by including SRP's mail order address in his five-star *Downbeat* review of *Live at Yale University*. It did well enough to support both a second pressing and a second volume with the remainder of the show. Looking back, in 2008, Graves explained the choice to self-produce at a matter of necessity, saying, "People didn't want to record the new jazz, so I said we can't wait around for someone to help us, we've got to help ourselves."[33]

However, in 1969, he had framed this as a specifically African-American self-reliance project. Graves believed the Jazz Composers Guild failed primarily because it included white people and that Black artists had distorted their work to suit the Downtown arts community: "For the sake of communicating with the white intellectuals, a lot of Black creativeness had to be thrown away." Similarly, he blamed the failure of previous Black-owned labels on their dependence on white-owned distributors and intended SRP to model an alternative.[34]

Calls for economic and cultural self-determination were common in this milieu. For example, Archie Shepp wrote in 1965, "Jazz is the product of the whites—the ofays—too often my enemy. It is the progeny of the blacks—my kinsmen. By this I mean: you own the music, and we make it," which Frank Kofsky expanded in 1970: "With very minor exceptions, it is whites who do own the major economic institutions of the jazz world—the booking agencies, recording companies, nightclubs, festivals, magazines, radio stations, etc. Blacks own nothing but their talents." Kofsky applied a Marxist analysis of African-Americans as an internal colony to the jazz art world.[35] However, arguments for self-reliance such as Graves's often grew from Black nationalism rather than Marxism. Graves had been part of Amiri Baraka's Black Arts Repertory Theater/School in 1965, a center of cultural nationalism, performing there with Pullen, with Albert Ayler, and with his own band, as well as teaching music classes.[36]

The second LP from the Yale concert was entitled *Nommo*. In German literary scholar Janheinz Jahn's 1958 book *Muntu: African Culture and the Western World*, which appeared in English in 1961, Nommo is a core principle of African philosophy: the life force, which shapes matter into conscious beings through the power of the word.[37] *Muntu* reached a wide audience as part of the Grove Press catalog, alongside many essential works for the 1950s and 1960s counterculture. Grove titles especially important to the African-American vanguard included Amiri Baraka's *The Dead Lecturer* and *Tales*, Franz Fanon's *The Wretched of the Earth* and *Black Skin, White Masks*, Jean Genet's *The Blacks*, Aimé Césaire's *A Season in the Congo*, and, most of all, *The Autobiography of Malcolm X*.[38]

Jahn was an ally of the Negritude movement; his work offered a construction of pan-African cultural unity that appealed to seekers in the diaspora. Besides Graves and Pullen's album, several Black Arts literary journals and anthologies also took the name Nommo, Oliver Lake's album title *Ntu: Point from which Creation Begins* almost certainly also came from Jahn, and Larry Neal's 1960s Philadelphia literary collective and Jemeel Moondoc's 1970s free jazz band were among the formations named Muntu.[39] *Muntu* was also the only reading Cecil Taylor assigned when he taught Black Music courses at the University of Wisconsin, Madison in 1971.[40]

Milford Graves first recorded as the timbalero in Montego Joe's Latin jazz band, then began playing drum set in free jazz groups. He initially approached the drum set as an enlarged timbale setup, allowing his legs to dance while he played interactively with his hands, then expanded his technique to use all four limbs independently to produce irregular polyrhythms.[41] Over the next fifty years, Graves theorized his work as channeling cosmic energy in relation to African and Afro-Cuban music, Zen Buddhism, Black ecstatic Christianity, and Santeria, and developed a system of alternative medicine related to energy, vibration, and rhythm. In performance he sought to alter his consciousness through drumming as a form of meditation or ritual and to present this to the audience as a shaman.[42] He wrote in the liner notes to *Nommo*:

> This music will cause a Mind-Challenge-Struggle within the self insofar that internal control is needed to adjust to the spontaneous forces. . . . If one tries to formulate our music, or listen to it with a biased mind towards rhythm-sound, he will only baffle himself. If you can let yourself react according to the natural principles of organic structure and free the mind of conventional laws of western music, you will cause less bewilderment within yourself.

Pullen and Graves's music sounds entirely improvised, "natural" and "organic," driven by energy rather than references to meter, tempo, tonality, or any of the other "conventional laws of western music." Pullen was accused of imitating Cecil Taylor in this early stage of his career, because he often played clusters (groups of adjacent pitches) and other textures associated with Taylor, but he did not employ Taylor's unit structures system or his anacrusis/area/plain forms. Pullen was a post-Taylor player, bringing some of his techniques to the challenge of completely open improvisation with Graves. In the 1970s and 1980s, he often applied the techniques and aesthetics of free jazz within song forms, working with George Adams, Hamiet Bluiett, Charles Mingus, David Murray, and his own groups, and revealed a strong background in blues and gospel, most dramatically in his organ performances on former James Brown saxophonist Maceo Parker's 1990 hit album *Roots Revisited*.

Wildflowers

In order to present their work despite the music industry's indifference and without its influence, free jazz musicians increasingly turned to artist-run labels in the footsteps of Saturn and Self-Reliance Productions, such as Ak-Ba (Charles Tyler), AltSax (Noah Howard), Asian Improv (Jon Jang and Francis Wong), Beak Doctor (Greg Goodman), Birth (Gunter Hampel), Braxton House and New Braxton House (Anthony Braxton), Center of the World (Alan Silva and Frank Wright), Centering (William Parker), Cryptogramophone (Jeff Gauthier), Edgetone (Rent Romus), Empire and Screwgun (Tim Berne), Ictus (Andrea Centazzo), Improvising Artists International (Paul Bley), Incus (Derek Bailey, Tony Oxley, and Evan Parker), Instant Composers Pool (Han Bennink, Willem Breuker, and Misha Mengelberg), JCOA (Carla Bley and Michael Mantler), Kabell (Wadada Leo Smith), Maya (Barry Guy and Maya Homburger), Mbari (Julius Hemphill), Metalanguage (Henry Kaiser and Larry Ochs), Nine Winds (Vinny Golia), Ogun (Harry Miller), Otic (Bobby Naughton), Passin' Thru (Oliver Lake), Pfmentum (Jeff Kaiser), Riti (Joe Morris), Skirl (Chris Speed), Survival (Rashied Ali), Tzadik (John Zorn), and Unit Core (Cecil Taylor). These goals also led them to form collectives and to produce their own performances. Three notable organizations, in three US cities—the Union of God's Musicians and Artists Ascension (UGMAA) in Los Angeles, the Association for the Advancement of

Creative Musicians (AACM) in Chicago, and the Black Artists Group (BAG) in St. Louis—differently addressed problems of economic and creative control in the 1960s and early 1970s.

In 1961, Horace Tapscott quit Lionel Hampton's band, frustrated by playing the same music every night to audiences who had come to party more than listen, and disturbed by the racism and danger he encountered on the road. Stepping back from an individual career, he chose to remain in South Los Angeles to make music in service of the community.[43] Tapscott named his band the Pan-Afrikan People's Arkestra, often shortened to PAPA or the Ark. He emulated Sun Ra's transformation of "orchestra" to "Arkestra," but noted that, "while he was thinking in terms of space, of an ark traveling through space, I was thinking in terms of a cultural safe house for music."[44] For Tapscott, the end of legal segregation had drained Black communities of resources as Black professionals moved to integrated suburbs, integrated schools did not teach Black history and culture, and the musicians' union stopped being a social and creative hub for Black musicians once it integrated.[45] The Ark was intended "to preserve the black arts in the community," to play music by Black composers, and to show the unity of Black music.[46] Tapscott formed a collective around the band, first named the Underground Musicians' Association, then the Union of God's Musicians and Artists Ascension.

As a community organization, the Ark mixed experienced jazz musicians, dedicated amateurs, and students. Tapscott also recruited African-American classical musicians, summoning them to play Black music in the heart of Los Angeles's Black community even if they were trained exclusively in European paradigms and had never improvised.[47] The Ark welcomed multiple levels and types of musicianship, emphasizing the community aspects of the music over the commercial.[48] UGMAA similarly united political elements. In the late 1960s and the 1970s, the Ark included members of the Black Panthers, US Organization, and the Nation of Islam and performed in support of these and other groups, as well as for the campaign of Tom Bradley, an ex-cop who became LA's first Black mayor in 1973.[49]

This work was not intended to advance the participants' careers but to serve the community. Performances were often at parks, schools, churches, or neighborhood centers. Admission was seldom charged and the musicians were rarely paid.[50] Some UGMAA musicians lived collectively in a series of buildings provided by patrons, who included actress Marla Gibbs from *The Jeffersons*.[51] Multiple applications for National

Endowment for the Arts grants failed, but UGMAA did receive federal job-training funds that enabled them to hire several members as office staff in the 1970s.[52] Tapscott himself was a member of the Supremes' touring band in the late 1960s and worked as a studio arranger, but was largely supported by his wife.[53]

Tapscott had bad experiences in the late 1960s recording for Contemporary, who insisted on using studio musicians instead of the Ark to play his compositions on Sonny Criss's *Sonny's Dream*, and for Flying Dutchman, who mixed his debut LP *The Giant Is Awakened* without his input.[54] He was so uninterested in recording that he only agreed to make that album after losing a band vote.[55] There are relatively few recordings of Tapscott and the Ark, almost all produced by fans-turned-patrons on their own specialized labels, including Toshiya Taenaka (Interplay Records), Tom Albach (Nimbus West), and Bertrand Gastaut (Dark Tree).[56]

While Tapscott encouraged members to compose and arrange for the Ark, he was unquestionably its musical and organizational center. In contrast, although Muhal Richard Abrams was the founder of Chicago's AACM, the group was run democratically and its members explored a very wide range of styles with their own bands. The Art Ensemble of Chicago was often perceived as the principal AACM group because they achieved the earliest and greatest recognition.[57]

The AACM focused on organizing performances. As member Anthony Braxton explained, "If you played what they thought was 'space' music or 'noise,' you couldn't get a gig. So, in 1966, '67, everybody turned around and discovered there was no work. It was the right moment for an organization like the AACM to happen."[58] They presented original music by their members in community centers, theaters, schools, and other spaces, often modeled on classical concerts with reserved seats, advance tickets, and printed programs, or incorporating multimedia elements, as in the early performance art "happenings" of John Cage, Allen Kaprow, and others.[59] These approaches challenged the status of jazz and violated expectations for its presentation. For example, one *Downbeat* editor complained in a review that the AACM held concerts at venues where audience members couldn't smoke or drink.[60]

Like UGMAA, the AACM's members had varied political and religious beliefs and affiliations. Also like UGMAA, the AACM was intentionally all-African-American so Black musicians could fully control their work.[61] During the 1960s, the AACM was funded entirely by member dues, choosing to not applying for government or foundation support in order to avoid depending on white-led institutions.[62]

However, as with ESP-Disk, UGMAA, and BYG, it was largely white patrons who had the resources to record this music. The first AACM albums, by Muhal Richard Abrams, Anthony Braxton, Joseph Jarman, Kalaparusha, and Roscoe Mitchell, appeared on Delmark Records, an established independent jazz and blues label run by Bob Koestler, who also owned the Jazz Record Mart. Chuck Nessa, who worked for Koestler at Delmark and the store, had persuaded him to record the AACM. After they fell out, he started his own Nessa label with a loan from his parents and released further albums by Mitchell, Fred Anderson, the Art Ensemble, Lester Bowie, Wadada Leo Smith, and Air (Henry Threadgill, Fred Hopkins, and Steve McCall).[63]

Lester Bowie told musicians in his hometown of St. Louis about the AACM, which helped inspire the formation of the Black Artists Group.[64] Unlike UGMAA and the AACM, BAG was not centered on music but included dance, theater, painting, and poetry, starting with their first project—a production of Jean Genet's *The Blacks*—in July 1968. BAG also differed from the other collectives in immediately seeking and winning foundation support. They partnered with Katherine Dunham's dance company to obtain 1968–69 grants from the Rockefeller and Danforth Foundations.[65] BAG and Dunham found a building whose owner charged them minimal rent, then used their grant money to remodel it for rehearsals, performances, and teaching.

Foundation support was not renewed for 1969–70 because BAG's work had been overtly political and centered in the African-American community, including supporting a rent strike in the nearby Pruitt-Igoe housing projects, while the grantmakers had expected them to cultivate a mixed audience and encourage "racial dialogue."[66] BAG's experience with foundation support seemed to bear out the AACM's reservations about relying on white institutional funding. Additionally, their building was sold and the new owner demanded market rate rent.[67]

As the name suggests, BAG was also exclusively African-American. However, BAG endorsed white improvisers James and Carol Marshall starting the Human Arts Association and the Human Arts Ensemble as integrated sister organizations to BAG.[68] BAG musicians regularly performed with the Human Arts Ensemble, often making up a majority of its members, and dual versions of the HAE sometimes coexisted, one led by the Marshalls and one by BAG/HAE drummer Charles Bobo Shaw.

Alternative venues and subsidies were also crucial to the London free music scene. Like many others, Evan Parker observed that this music required a dedicated space, not a bar or a club.[69] The network of players around the Spontaneous Music Ensemble, including Parker, Derek Bailey, John Stevens, Paul Rutherford, Barry Guy, and Trevor Watts, were able to use the Little Theatre Club at no cost six nights a week, after the club's plays finished.[70] The music was freed from the demands of audiences and the marketplace. Parker also recalls that food was cheap and rent low in Britain in the late 1960s, so it was easy to survive as a musician.[71] Additionally, the British enjoyed a more functional social safety net than their American counterparts: Rutherford and bassist Roberto Bellatalla both describe going on the dole to support their creative work rather than taking day jobs.[72]

Economic circumstances also drew free jazz musicians to New York in the 1970s. Manufacturing began decisively leaving Manhattan in 1958, when the Port of New York moved across the Hudson to New Jersey to embrace container shipping, making industrial buildings available for other uses and starting the live/work loft phenomenon.[73] These large, unimproved, and inexpensive spaces were very attractive to artists. In 1961 jazz fan Dan Serro rented a 2,400 square foot loft at 9 Great Jones Street for $125 monthly, where he hosted a Don Cherry performance mentioned by Amiri Baraka in a *Downbeat* piece entitled "Coffee Shop and Loft Jazz." This may have been the first time the phrase "loft jazz" appeared in print.[74]

In 1972 Ornette Coleman released *Friends and Neighbors: Live at Prince Street*, recorded in 1970 at his loft.[75] Coleman's space, subsequently named Artists' House, was one of the first of many musician-run loft venues, such as Studio Rivbea (Sam Rivers), Ali's Alley (Rashied Ali), Studio WIS (Warren Smith), Studio We (James DuBoise), Studio Infinity (David Murray and Stanley Crouch), and Ladies Fort (Jo Lee Wilson).[76] "Loft jazz" became a popular description of the music in the 1970s, although musicians balked at its implications. As Muhal Richard Abrams warned, "You must watch the term 'loft jazz' because it's too limiting. We didn't come to New York to play in lofts; we came to make a living. But an audience can start, and grow until it gets too big for the lofts and the music moves to another level."[77]

When New York City hosted the Newport Jazz Festival in 1972, a group of loft-based performers and presenters including Ali, DuBoise, Rivers, Milford Graves, Noah Howard, and Juma Sultan formed the New York Musicians Organization to demand Newport give Black musicians significant control of the festival and Black community organizations the majority of its profits. After these demands were rejected, the NYMO staged an impressive counter-festival, whose opening night featured sets by Rivers, Ali, Anthony Braxton, and Andrew Hill, and which included more acts at more venues than Newport. This show of strength led to Newport sponsoring the next year's NYMO festival alongside their own.[78]

Cheap or free housing allowed musicians to focus on their art.[79] In 1969, Burton Greene lived rent-free at the space that became Studio We in exchange for providing basic security and maintenance.[80] When David S. Ware, Alan Braufman, and Cooper Moore moved to New York from Boston in 1973, they rented a four-story building at 501 Canal St. for a total of $550 monthly. They used the first floor to rehearse and perform, Ware and Braufman shared the second, Cooper-Moore had the third to himself, because he was the property manager, and drummer Jimmy Hopps took the fourth.[81] Musicians including Tim Berne, Karen Borca, Mark Helias, Michael Gregory Jackson, Bern Nix, William Parker, and Mark Whitecage have similar stories about how affordable housing enabled them to live in Manhattan among a community of artists, surviving by working less than half-time in simple jobs such as messenger or delivery person or by playing a couple of mainstream or pop gigs each month.[82] In 1977, the Manhattan Plaza apartments opened in Midtown, offering Section 8 subsidized housing specifically to full-time performing artists, including numerous jazz musicians.[83]

These opportunities brought many musicians from the regional collectives to Manhattan in the 1970s, including Muhal Richard Abrams, Lester Bowie, Chico Freeman, Fred Hopkins, Kalaparusha, George Lewis, Steve McCall, Amina Claudia Myers, and Henry Threadgill from the AACM and Hamiet Bluiett, Joseph Bowie, Baikida Carroll, Julius Hemphill, Oliver Lake, and J. D. Parran from BAG.[84] Some Los Angeles transplants came through UGMAA, such as Arthur Blythe, Will Connell, and Lawrence "Butch" Morris, while others were connected through Stanley Crouch's unrecorded California band Black Music Infinity, such as Mark Dresser, David Murray, and James Newton.[85]

In 1976 Casablanca Records recorded a week of shows at Sam Rivers's Studio Rivbea loft. Of the twenty groups on the five *Wildflowers* LPs produced from these sessions, eight were led by veterans of the Guild/ESP/Impulse era: Marion Brown, Dave Burrell, Andrew Cyrille, Byard Lancaster, Jimmy Lyons, Ken McIntyre, Sunny Murray, and Rivers himself. Five were led by AACM members: Anthony Braxton, Kalaparusha, Roscoe Mitchell, Wadada Leo Smith, and Threadgill, while three were led by BAG members: Bluiett, Hemphill, and Lake. David Murray was the only Angeleno, guitarist Michael Gregory Jackson was from New Haven, and the remaining two leaders were Sun Ra trumpeter Ahmed Abdullah and expatriate pianist Randy Weston.[86]

While the loft scene attracted international attention, it remained economically marginal. Ali's Alley was typical in giving musicians the money collected at the door, while the house kept the proceeds from food and drink sales. However, some lofts also charged artists to use the space or took a share of the admissions. Studio Rivbea was the only loft offering performers a guarantee and could do that only when it had National Endowment for the Arts and New York State Arts Council grants.[87] Julius Hemphill recalled that loft concerts often drew in the low double-digits.[88] Seating at 501 Canal Street consisted of thirty folding chairs.[89] More established artists such as Jimmy Lyons, Marion Brown, and Charles Tyler could expect sixty to eighty listeners.[90] However, a growing European summer festival circuit enabled players to reach larger audiences, record for European independent labels such as hatHut and Black Saint/Soul Note, and bring home money to help them through the rest of the year.[91]

Jazz historian Michael Heller describes the loft jazz community in terms of "pay, play, place, and race:" financial, aesthetic, geographic, and racial connections.[92] All four of these broke down in the early 1980s. Although New York had legalized live/work spaces for artists in 1964, landlords often preferred to rent lofts cheaply as studios rather than bringing them up to residential standards, though it was tacitly understood people would live there. This gave landlords tremendous leverage. Some offered cheap or free space in exchange for the residents upgrading their units then reported them for illegally living in commercial space when the work was done.[93] Even tenants with ethical landlords were often displaced by the cycle of gentrification in which musicians and artists move into a neighborhood and make it so fashionable that most of them can no longer afford to live there.[94] Gentrification disrupted the "pay" and "place" of the loft jazz community, while the "play" and "race" elements were challenged by the emergence of Wynton Marsalis and the Young Lions movement, on one hand, which presented alternative visions of jazz history and Black identity, and of a significantly white and rock-inspired Downtown improvised music scene centered on artists such as Eugene Chadbourne, Fred Frith, Bill Laswell, Arto Lindsay, Elliott Sharp, and John Zorn, on the other.[95]

Uptown and Downtown

Free jazz musicians were not the only ones taking advantage of the affordable live/work spaces in New York in the 1970s. As Will Hermes recounts in *Love Goes to Buildings on Fire*, the same circumstances that produced loft jazz also fostered the development of punk, disco, salsa, minimalism, and hip-hop.[96] Before Amiri Baraka wrote about free jazz loft shows in *Downbeat*, Yoko Ono, LaMonte Young, and Richard Maxfield were organizing Fluxus events at her loft, presenting experimental music that overlapped with what would become performance and conceptual art.[97]

This strand of underground experimental composition continued through the emergence of the drone and pattern-based minimalism of Young, Terry Riley, Philip Glass, and Steve Reich into the 1970s. The Kitchen, which began in the kitchen of the Mercer Arts Center and moved to a Soho loft in 1974, became the premier venue for composers interested in alternatives to European modernism, which came to be known as Downtown music (the lineage of John Cage) in contrast to Uptown (the lineage of Arnold Schoenberg).[98] While Uptown composers produced precise atonal scores, Downtown admitted improvisation, multimedia, and influences from non-European and popular music.[99] The Kitchen's music curators in the 1970s—Rhys Chatham, Arthur Russell, and Garrett List—were all active Downtown performer/composers and booked rock bands who shared their sensibility, such as the Modern Lovers, Talking Heads, and Theoretical Girls, as well as free jazz musicians including the Art Ensemble of Chicago, Anthony Braxton, Julius Hemphill, the Human Arts Ensemble, Oliver Lake, George Lewis, Archie Shepp, Wadada Leo Smith, and Cecil Taylor.[100] The Kitchen's 1979 New Music/New York festival was a defining event for the Downtown scene and included Lewis, Don Cherry, and Jeanne Lee. It continued until 1990 as the New Music America festival, held in a different city each year, creating a national platform for Downtown artists and aesthetics.

In September 1980 George Lewis became the Kitchen's fourth music curator, the first African-American in that role. His first presentation was electronic musician Tom Hamilton in a duo with BAG clarinetist J. D. Parran on the 8th, followed by John Zorn's game piece "Jai Alai" on the 9th.[101] In contrast to the subsistence economy of the lofts, the Kitchen's 1980 budget was over half a million dollars, supported by grants. While loft performers often were only paid a share of the door and their shows promoted by flyers in a handful of record stores, the Kitchen was able to offer composers commissions and performers guarantees, plus professional publicity and advertising. Lewis's intention was to share these resources with Black artists who had rarely if ever had this level of support in the US. He also intended to challenge the color line in experimental music, not just to admit free jazz as an alternative experimental music, but to show that what separated many of its practitioners from the post-Cage avant-garde was frequently context and complexion rather than content, working towards what he called a "nonracialized" experimentalism.[102]

Reviewing the 1964 October Revolution in *Downbeat*, Dan Morgenstern had observed that the existing jazz art world could not support free jazz, that it required and deserved the same foundation and government support as other noncommercial art, a position supported by Bill Dixon.[103] Proximity to other experimental artists in Greenwich Village both encouraged jazz musicians to see themselves as their peers and exposed how little access Black art and Black artists had to institutional sources of prestige and funding.[104] For example, as A. B. Spellman observed, Cecil Taylor faced the lack of literal or conceptual space for "Black serious music."[105] Black music was expected to be entertainment and experimentalism white. Taylor was much more at the mercy of show business than John Cage. Free jazz made space for "Black serious music" through an inside/outside strategy: both creating alternative labels, venues, and organizations and claiming a share of existing ones.

While BAG and the Black Arts Repertory Theater/School received early grants from programs for community uplift and education, cultural grantmakers were slower to recognize the music. Ornette Coleman was the first jazz musician to win a Guggenheim Fellowship, in 1967; he won a second in 1974.[106] The National Endowment for the Arts began funding jazz in the late 1960s, but very modestly. Their 1971 budget included $50,000 for jazz, compared to $3,500,000 for classical music.[107]

White-led free jazz organizations initially had greater success navigating the grant process. For example, Free Life Communications, a cooperative led by Dave Liebman and Bob Moses, was one of the first lofts to receive funding, and the Jazz Composers Orchestra Association, Carla Bley and Michael Mantler's spinoff from the Jazz Composers Guild, won five NEA grants between 1970 and 1976.[108] Bley and Mantler also organized the New Music Distribution Service, a grant-supported clearinghouse for independent and artist-owned record labels, particularly free jazz and Downtown music. NMDS sold LPs directly to listeners and wholesale to stores from 1972 until 1990, when it and many of the labels it carried were undone by the shift to CDs.[109]

Larry Neal and A. B. Spellman became arts administrators in the 1970s, bringing their experiences in the Black Arts Movement into the nonprofit establishment.[110] Muhal Richard Abrams began serving on NEA panels judging grant applications in the mid-1970s and similarly attempted to reform their process. For example, before Abrams, the NEA had required that jazz proposals include sample scores in standard notation, which excluded artists who worked with graphics, text, and other alternative systems, like many AACM members, while scores accompanying classical applications could be in any format.[111]

When the MacArthur Foundation launched their fellowship program, popularly known as the "Genius Grants," in 1981, Uptown composers such as Milton Babbitt and Charles Wuorinen were the first musicians recognized. However, artists associated with free jazz have dominated since the 1990s, including Anthony Braxton, Ornette Coleman, Vijay Iyer, Steve Lacy, Mary Halvorson, George Lewis, Tyshawn Sorey, Cecil Taylor, Ken Vandermark, and John Zorn. Similarly, while the first jazz musician to win the Pulitzer Prize for Music was Wynton Marsalis in 1997, the subsequent jazz-related winners have all been from the avant-garde: Ornette Coleman (2007), Henry Threadgill (2016), and Anthony Davis (2020).

Free jazz musicians were also increasingly able to turn to academic jobs for support. Black Arts Movement theorists often centered music in their conception of culture, which encouraged universities to hire free jazz musicians as faculty in their newly formed Black Studies programs, notably Archie Shepp at the State University of New York at Buffalo, then the University of Massachusetts at Amherst, Cecil Taylor at the University of Wisconsin at Madison, Antioch College, and Glassboro State College, and Sun Ra at the University of California at Berkeley and San Francisco State University. Others were hired by music departments, beginning with Bill Dixon and Milford Graves at Bennington.[112] They were followed by Geri Allen, Karl Berger, Anthony Braxton, Taylor Ho Bynum, Andrew Cyrille, Anthony Davis, Mark Dresser, Marty Ehrlich, James Fei, Charles Gayle, Vinny Golia, Charlie Haden, Mary Halvorson, Vijay Iyer, Steve Lacy, Steve Lehman, George Lewis, Raphe Malik, Ken McIntyre, Myra Melford, Nicole Mitchell, Roscoe Mitchell, Joe Morris, James Newton, Tomeka Reid, Sam Rivers, Wadada Leo Smith, Glenn Spearman, and many others, initially at small, open-minded, Downtown-friendly art schools and liberal arts colleges like Bennington, such as Mills, Wesleyan, and the California Institute of the Arts (CalArts).[113] However, in 2004, Lewis was hired at Columbia, historically the center of Uptown composition. In 2013, Geri Allen became chair of jazz studies at the University of Pittsburgh, the only jazz program offering a doctorate, and she was succeeded in 2019 by Nicole Mitchell.

6

Ancient to the Future

Ken Vandermark has argued that free jazz existed as a movement from Ornette Coleman's New York debut in 1959 until John Coltrane's death in 1967, then became a style, a defined idiom rather than an emergent one.[1] However, this approach to the historiography of free jazz excludes an enormous amount of work, from Alice Coltrane and Pharoah Sanders to the AACM, European free improvisation, and Vandermark's own career. Following Vandermark's criteria, one could discuss spiritual jazz, the AACM, and European free improvisation as their own movements and as groups of successive movements, since each of them is now multigenerational, but a more inclusive approach allows for tracing the spread and development of ideas like energy music, jazz as a spiritual practice, and conducted improvisation, and also recognizes the range of the music made just between 1959 and 1967, from John Coltrane's "Giant Steps" to *Ascension*, Sun Ra's "India" to *Atlantis*, Cecil Taylor's *Love for Sale* to *Unit Structures*, and so on. This concluding chapter proposes two alternate narratives of the endurance and relevance of free jazz.

A Jackson in Your House

The Art Ensemble of Chicago's debut album, *A Jackson in Your House*, recorded in Paris in June 1969, was one of the first releases on the BYG label. The Art Ensemble formed through the AACM and all four players were multi-instrumentalists. The saxophonists carried woodwinds from bass saxophone to piccolo and everyone employed a variety of percussion and "little instruments" to expand their sonic palette and, in 1969, to cover for the group's temporary lack of a drummer. They also incorporated poetry and other spoken and sung vocals, costumes, and stage business ranging from facing east in nondenominational prayer to comedy skits.

A Jackson in Your House opens with the title track, a simple march-like melody based entirely on the major scale, composed by Roscoe Mitchell. Albert Ayler frequently used similar themes, such as his "Spirits Rejoice" and "Truth Is Marching In," to create energy and drive ecstatic improvisations, but the Art Ensemble approaches this tune quite differently. They play the first eight bars of the melody in unison, then dissolve into a chaotic bicycle horn ensemble. Mitchell alternates fragments of the melody played on dinner chimes with passages on unpitched little instruments, then bassist Malachi Favors introduces the root-fifth bass line and cues the full theme. They play it three times. The first time through, Lester Bowie's trumpet and Joseph Jarman's soprano saxophone are in unison, while Mitchell stays on percussion, using woodblocks to evoke the sound of early jazz. On the repeat, Mitchell sings about his cat Jackson in an affected comic voice, accompanied by trumpet, bass, bicycle horns, and laughter. On the third repetition, Favors reinforces the early jazz feel by adding upbeat slaps to the bass line and the horns collectively improvise close to the melody. The music pauses, but the performance continues. After some mumbled conversation, Jarman says, "Come on, let's play some blues!" Mitchell launches into a clarinet solo, ironically on rhythm changes rather than the blues, as the group maintains the early jazz idiom with a bass line in two, Jarman playing a frequently choked ride cymbal, and Bowie joining in melodic collective improvising. Jarman also continues his commentary, exclaiming, "Tryin' to play some blues! You playin' some jazz there, huh?"[2]

Here, in the first minutes of their first album, the Art Ensemble introduce several new attitudes to jazz. There has always been humor in jazz, ranging from musicians' inside jokes to broad comedy, but "A Jackson in Your House" is strikingly silly. It's full of bicycle horns, woodblocks, and funny voices; Mitchell warns that his cat "will scratch you on the rump." However, the second track of *A Jackson in Your House*, "Get in Line," quickly shifts the mood. It begins with the identical root-fifth bass line, in the same key, and similarly breaks off into a section of little instruments with Jarman shouting, but it immediately becomes clear that he is playing a racist drill sergeant and that this piece is about militarism and war. All four members of the Art Ensemble were army veterans.[3] The continuity created by the bass line suggests a narrative where the happy crew from "A Jackson in Your House" are drafted and sent to boot camp en route to Vietnam. Juxtaposing these pieces also demonstrates that even the simplest musical element, such as an oompah bass line, can alternately convey silliness and sadism. These emotions, and the multivalence of musical signs, are seldom explored in jazz.

It is also novel that "A Jackson in Your House" incorporates its own critique. The musicians heckle and laugh at their performance throughout, and this theatrical element seems as composed as the sequence of themes and improvisations. Jarman's comments about jazz and blues are essential: he is an embedded spectator, praising the band when they approach his expectations of jazz. The record includes an audible performance of jazz listening, parrying and parodying anticipated responses. It asks if it is jazz before the listener can. This reflexivity is a crucial innovation, as is the use of stylistic pastiche. Previously, artists seldom cited historic styles in their work. For example, when Miles Davis recorded "Basin Street Blues" and "Baby Won't You Please Come Home" in 1963, he, Herbie Hancock, Ron Carter, and Tony Williams approached them as if they were contemporary compositions, not overtly referring to the iconic recordings by Louis Armstrong and Bessie Smith from decades earlier. Davis and his band played the music, not the history of the music. In contrast, the Art Ensemble's style is polyglot. Their catalog includes funk ("Theme de Yo-Yo"), bebop ("We Bop"), evocations of John Coltrane ("Onedaruth"), Charles Mingus ("Charlie M"), and Miles Davis ("Dreaming of the Master"), reggae ("Ja"), complex atonal themes ("Nonaah"), groove and texture-oriented percussion ensembles ("Bush Magic"), free improvisation, uncategorizable theatrical pieces, poetry, assorted cover songs, and so on.

As Joseph Jarman put it in 1969, "We play the blues, we play jazz, rock; Spanish, Gypsy, and African music; classical music, contemporary European music, voodoo. Everything, really—because, ultimately, we play 'music.' We create sounds, period."[4] Lester Bowie similarly said, "We're free to express ourselves in any so-called idiom, to draw from any source, to deny any limitation. We weren't restricted to bebop, free jazz, Dixieland, theater or poetry. We could put it all together. We could sequence it any way we like it. It was all up to us."[5]

The Art Ensemble specifically performed under the motto Bowie and Favors created for the AACM—"Great Black Music: Ancient to the Future"—often displaying it on a banner or a drum head.[6] This slogan generated some controversy and misunderstanding. At least one French critic in 1969 interpreted it as espousing a separatist cultural nationalism.[7] In 1975, AACM member Anthony Braxton, whose career was dogged from the beginning by charges that his music was "not Black enough," especially in comparison to the Art Ensemble, complained the slogan was racist.[8]

Judging by the words and music of the Art Ensemble, neither of these critiques was accurate. Paul Steinbeck described "Great Black Music" as "at once a pan-African theory of culture, an expression of diasporic consciousness, and a radical declaration that black music could be whatever the Art Ensemble wanted it to be."[9] It asserts the centrality of Africa to civilization and the resulting interrelationship of cultures, especially those of the Black Atlantic, particularly through the pervasive influence of African diasporic musics, as well as declaring Black artists' creative freedom. In contrast to the prescriptive "Black is/Black ain't" discourse that vexed Braxton and others, the Art Ensemble entitled a 1970 track "Certain Blacks (Do What They Wanna)."[10] Mitchell's austere microtonal soprano saxophone solo "S II Examples" is Great Black Music, as are Bowie's covers of the Spice Girls and Puccini with his band Brass Fantasy.

Besides centering the African diaspora in music history, "Great Black Music: Ancient to the Future" defines Black music as a living tradition. In Bowie's words, "We can be free to interpret everything that's ever been played, and things that have never been played."[11] By interpreting the freedom of free jazz as a freedom to include overt historical and style references and to explore the most esoteric and the most prosaic materials, the Art Ensemble and the AACM claimed a future in which the music endures by expanding. Furthermore, the reference to the future anticipates the artistic movement known as Afrofuturism, which includes AACM flutist Nicole Mitchell and Art Ensemble collaborator Moor Mother. It not only declares that there will be a future for Black music, but that, in the words of Afrofuturist artist Alisha Wormsley, "There are Black People in the Future."[12]

At the same time, as the AACM and the Art Ensemble turned fifty and Roscoe Mitchell eighty, their projects became more reflexive and retrospective. Mitchell's *Bells for the Southside* (2017) combined four of his trios into a nonet for a fiftieth anniversary AACM concert, invoking the Art Ensemble by using that group's iconic percussion and little instruments setups. His albums *Discussions* (2017), *Ride the Wind*

(2018), *Littlefield Concert Hall, Mills College, March 19–20, 2018* (2019), and *Distant Radio Transmission* (2019) are based on trio improvisations with keyboardist Craig Taborn and drummer Kikanju Baku, transcribed from the albums *Conversations I* and *Conversations II* (2014) and arranged to be replayed by large groups with soloists adding new improvisations, while on *We are on the Edge* (2019), Mitchell and drummer Famoudou Don Moye convened a new eighteen member Art Ensemble to interpret new and classic material for the group's fiftieth anniversary.

Despite the Art Ensemble's longevity and influence, few other musicians have performed their material. Neither the record collector sites allmusic.com and discogs.com nor the library union catalog worldcat.org list any recording of "A Jackson in Your House" by any other artist. The original version is a document of a performance as much as a version of a composition; its theatrical and conceptual elements seem essential and irreproducible. When the Art Ensemble played it live, they did not attempt to duplicate the recording, its episodic format, or specific events from it, but used the principal theme and the associated idea of jazz anachronisms as elements of larger-scale mostly improvised performances.[13]

Mitchell's "People in Sorrow," a short slow minor-key melody, is a rare example of an Art Ensemble theme taken up by other players. On the original recording, also from Paris 1969, it occupies an entire LP, beginning in near-silence with little instruments and gradually building to full force over forty minutes.[14] The players stay close to the theme throughout, with no real foreground solos, but they do not play the complete melody until the start of the second album side. Two notable interpretations of "People in Sorrow" by other artists recontextualize Mitchell's theme; neither retains the slow development of the original.

In 1975, Mototeru Takagi, the saxophonist on Masahiko Togashi's *We Now Create*, recorded a fourteen-minute version accompanied by bass and drums in a theme-solos-theme format, played with intense post-Ayler energy. In contrast, for a tribute to Mitchell at the 2011 Angel City Jazz Festival, issued on CD and DVD as *For People in Sorrow*, drummer Alex Cline assembled an eleven-piece band, augmented by a poetic invocation, prerecorded Buddhist chants, and a conductor, for an hour-long performance that alternated statements of the theme with free improvisations by subgroups ranging from string trio to slide guitar and bass drum to cornet and rhythm section.

Dogon A.D.

While the Art Ensemble models a future for free jazz as a radically inclusive creative practice, their compositions may be too specific or eccentric to be played by anyone else without major revision. In contrast, Julius Hemphill's "Dogon A.D." has entered the repertoire of several contemporary artists and suggests a narrative where free jazz becomes part of a new common practice.

Hemphill recorded the *Dogon A.D.* album, plus "The Hard Blues," released as half of his second LP *'Coon Bid'ness*, in one session in February 1972. He played alto saxophone and flute, joined by Baikida Carroll on trumpet, Abdul Wadud on cello, and Philip Wilson on drums, with baritone saxophonist Hamiet Bluiett added on "The Hard Blues."

The release history of *Dogon A.D.* illustrates several trends in free jazz as a business. It first appeared on Hemphill's label Mbari, in a pressing of 500.[15] Arista Records reissued it in 1977 as part of their short-lived Freedom series, along with fifty other import and independent free jazz titles. This edition was approximately 4,000 copies.[16] Once it went out of print the album was only available secondhand and through file sharing until International Phonograph reissued it in 2011 (1,500 CDs) and 2016 (1,000 LPs). These editions are now sold out and it has not been licensed for downloading or streaming. This route from a DIY release to a corporate reissue to a boutique reissue tracks the music's movement from the underground to the spotlight and back, as well as from Black Arts Movement DIY to a corporation's aesthetic indulgence/tax write-off to an audience of hipsters and collectors. It also demonstrates that even work of great acclaim and influence can exist in a series of modest editions adding up to only a few thousand copies.

Hemphill discussed multiple aspects of his interest in the Dogon people of Mali. Elements of their belief system were already in circulation in the Black Arts Movement through the popular book *Muntu: An Outline of the New African Culture*, and painter Oliver Jackson, a fellow member of BAG, gave Hemphill Marcel Griaule's *Conversations with Ogotemmêli: An Introduction to Dogon Religious Ideas*.[17] He also was attracted to the visual qualities of Dogon sculpture and dance.[18] His friend Donald Suggs had opened the Alexander-Suggs Gallery of African Art in St. Louis in 1970, so Hemphill was able to view some Dogon pieces close-up. This was probably also where he saw the autumn 1971 issue of *African Arts*, which included the article "Contemporary Adapted Dances of the Dogon," by Pascal Imperato.[19] Hemphill was inspired by this description of the Dogon's choice to create "adapted" versions of their traditional dances to perform for tourists by obscuring their religious meanings and incorporating European elements. He saw this as generous and open, as well as calculated, a savvy compromise with Europe and modernity: "I found it to be very impressive that they would get together and plan this strategy, being that the dances go back hundreds of years."[20] Hemphill described his composition "Dogon A.D. [adaptive dance]" as "a small contribution toward their control of their stuff," drawing a parallel between their self-determination efforts and those of BAG and similar Black Arts Movement projects.[21] These connections were clear in the first known performance of "Dogon A.D," which was at the BAG building, accompanying dancers from Katherine Dunham's company. The musicians wore African robes and the performance area included Dogon sculpture and other African art objects, which the dancers used as props.[22]

Hemphill was inspired by *Conversations with Ogotemmêli's* descriptions both of Dogon beliefs and of the relationship between the French anthropologist Griaule and the Dogon sage Ogotemmêli. As Hemphill put it, "Ogotemmêli bullshitted him for thirty years about what was going on. Then another guy—they decided to reveal a little more of it."[23] The dynamics of concealing and revealing between the anthropologist and his informants and in the adaptation of the Dogon dance for public performance resonate with those between artists, audiences, and scholars, and between the intersecting communities of free jazz, as well as W. E. B. DuBois's idea of double-consciousness. Bill Shoemaker describes "Dogon A.D." as "rural and urban and, ultimately, American and African."[24] None of these qualities is the essential truth of the piece; they are all sonically constructed and invoked.

Philip Wilson begins "Dogon A.D" marking the eleven-beat rhythm as two groups of four and a group of three, so each bar sounds like it is composed of three asymmetrical beats. Later, during Hemphill's solo, he adds backbeats on the third and seventh notes, treating the eleven as a bar of 4/4 with three eighth notes appended. The written bass line generally leaves every other bar silent and stays close to the tonic chord and the 4-4-3 pattern, but Wadud briefly chooses to imply the subdominant or play parts of the melody in harmony with the horns. Under the solos, he continues to leave a lot of open space and bases his accompaniment on a figure from the melody rather than the written bass line, creating harmonic ambiguity in what is essentially a one-chord groove. Wadud also adds to the raw feel by using a noisy bow attack. He did not use an amplifier at this time and seems to have played very hard in order to match the volume of the horns and drums.[25]

Hemphill's melody begins with bluesy pentatonic phrases and hints at a move from the tonic to the subdominant in the second phrase, characteristic of the blues, but the bass line stays on the tonic there and the melody goes its own way. The repetitive groove is Hemphill's impression of Dogon music and of the blues, not a literal imitation of either, while the theme proposes a range of options for the soloists, presenting funky, oblique, and abstract material.[26] Hemphill and Carroll both employ all these possibilities in their solos.

On Hemphill's 1984 recording with the JAH Band, not a reggae band but named for his initials, bass guitarist Steuart Liebig takes a more bass-like approach to accompanying the soloists, frequently playing root-root-minor third on the downbeats of the 4-4-3 pattern, as Wadud did at the beginning of the original. When guitarist Nels Cline enters for the second solo, using a highly processed tone, and Liebig switches from fingerstyle to slapping, they evoke the 1980s edition of King Crimson. This is a version of free jazz that admits whatever the players bring to it and that can also become part of other varieties of musical practice.

Saxophonist Marty Ehrlich formed the Rites Quartet with the same reeds, trumpet, cello, and drums instrumentation Hemphill used on *Dogon A.D.* and 1980's *Flat-Out Jump Suite* to perform Hemphill's repertoire and new work by Ehrlich. The version of "Dogon A.D." on their 2009 album *Things Have Got to Change* recreates the original during the theme, with cellist Eric Friedlander even emulating Wadud's rough attack. Friedlander begins each horn solo playing the roots and downbeats, then moves to Wadud's riff. Ehrlich and trumpeter James Zollar do not imitate Hemphill and Carroll in their solos but play in their own voices.

Danish drummer Stefan Pasborg's Odessa 5, the Albuquerque/Los Angeles trio Do Tell, and the Italian duo Pospaghemme are all horn and percussion ensembles. On the Odessa 5's 2008 recording of "Dogon A.D," Pasborg stays close to Wilson's beat while tuba and trombone play the root-minor third figure and alto saxophone and trumpet use the melody to frame a bluesy trumpet solo. On Do Tell's 2015 recording, drummer Dave Wayne initially interprets the beat as funk with snare ruffs and hi-hat accents, then moves to the ride cymbal and a more open postbop feel under Dan Clucas's cornet solo, while tubaist Mark Weaver holds the bass riff before taking a long open solo. Pospaghemme's 2009 version opens with a free improvisation on little instruments and banjo, then the drums slip into the beat. After an exposition of the theme, with the baritone saxophone also covering the bass line when possible, it abruptly returns to the texture of the opening.

On *Historicity*, also from 2009, pianist Vijay Iyer's trio includes "Dogon A.D." alongside tunes by Andrew Hill, Stevie Wonder, M.I.A., Ronnie Foster, and Leonard Bernstein, as well as three originals, proposing a personal canon mixing Broadway, free jazz, hip-hop, and R and B. Iyer creates a harmonization for the theme, while bassist Stephen Crump plays arco when interpreting Wadud's part and pizzicato when inventing his own. For the improvising, the band breaks up the eleven, playing across bar lines and the 4-4-3 grouping. This freer approach to odd meters reflects their integration into common practice and Iyer's special focus on them, drawing on both his apprenticeship with Steve Coleman and the rhythmic approaches associated with his Indian heritage. The Miles Davis and Bill Evans groups of the 1960s established that rhythm sections did not need to express downbeats, chord changes, or sectional divisions as overtly as had been standard, and subsequent ensembles applied this technique to increasingly complex material. Iyer's trio handles eleven as obliquely as their predecessors did 4/4.

The Italian band Roots Magic recorded "Dogon A.D." on their 2017 album *Last Kind Words*, along with versions of Hemphill's "Hattie Wall," Henry Threadgill's "Bermuda Blues," Marion Brown's "November Cotton Flower," and Roscoe Mitchell's "Old." Like Iyer, their selection of covers both recognizes their influences and presents them in their own style. For Roots Magic, this means a heavier, tighter, and more hook-oriented arrangement. The bass plays a set line throughout, the drummer almost always plays the second group of four as a backbeat, and each horn solo begins softly and rises to a wailing climax. One new element, borrowed from Hemphill's "The Hard Blues," is that after the theme statement, the horns freak out for four bars, then reunite to repeat a phrase from the theme to launch the solos.

Salim Washington's 2018 version on his *Dogon Revisited* takes an opposite direction from Roots Magic, heightening the dissonances in the theme statement and turning the solos into collective improvisations, with Tyshawn Sorey's cymbal crashes every two or four bars the only obvious markers of the meter.

Broken Shadows is an all-star free jazz tribute band, focused on the compositions of Fort Worth, Texas, natives Ornette Coleman, Dewey

Redman, and Hemphill, and Oklahoman bassist Charlie Haden. Saxophonists Tim Berne and Chris Speed, who had a long collaboration in Berne's band Bloodcount, front the bass and drums team from the Bad Plus. Their 2018 studio and 2019 live recordings of "Dogon A.D." stay close to Hemphill's original, although they replace trumpet with tenor saxophone and cello with bass, and drummer Chris King plays the beat fluidly while presenting the eleven-beat meter and the 4-4-3 division more explicitly than Sorey.

The Bad Plus debuted in 2000 as a piano trio. Their music didn't deal with free jazz but instead seemed to extend Charles Lloyd, Gary Burton, and Keith Jarrett's late 1960s work, which covered rock and pop songs without condescension and admitted rock rhythms while preserving the instrumentation and dynamics of mainstream jazz. However, joined by Berne, soprano saxophonist Sam Newsome, and cornetist Ron Miles, they toured in 2014 and 2015 playing the music from Ornette Coleman's *Science Fiction* album.

Tim Berne and Marty Ehrlich were Hemphill's protégés; both have recorded his work in multiple contexts, and Ehrlich coordinated the institutionalization of his archive at NYU, with extensive subsequent score and CD publications.[27] Broken Shadows and the Rites Quartet are specifically tribute projects and thus emulate the original recording more than other versions. Berne and Ehrlich's choices of other Hemphill covers suggest the specific aspects of his work most connected to theirs: Ehrlich played "The Painter," a flute feature originally recorded on *Dogon A.D*, on his 1991 *Emergency Peace* album, and his own music often reflects the direct melodic and emotional qualities of Hemphill pieces like this and "Georgia Blue." In contrast, Berne covered the entire first side of Hemphill's 1975 *'Coon Bid'ness* LP as a medley on Bloodcount's 1995 *Lowlife: The Paris Concert*, a parallel to his own extended episodic pieces, which often frame each improvising section with new composed material and present each soloist in a different setting. For example, "Bro-ball," from Bloodcount's 1996 album *Unwound*, begins with a fast quirky theme played in unison by Berne and bassist Michael Formanek. Chris Speed enters with a counterline on the repeat and takes the first solo, accompanied by bass and drums, all freely using material from the theme. On cue Berne and Formanek play an odd-meter unison riff to energize the end of Speed's solo, then the group plays a second theme and Berne and drummer Jim Black play a free duo that becomes a drum solo. The drum solo continues over a third ensemble theme, then concludes over a vamp.

Human Feel, Speed and Black's quartet with guitarist Kurt Rosenwinkel and saxophonist Andrew D'Angelo, uses similar forms. D'Angelo's "Sich Reped" (almost an anagram of "Chris Speed"), from their 1994 album *Welcome to Malapesta*, is in three two-minute sections. The first is entirely composed, with odd meter loops, fast unison lines, and many sudden tempo changes. This abruptly shifts to the second, a softer and slower melody played in canon, which stops cold for an improvised saxophone duet with both players occasionally referring to a short composed riff, playing it to accompany the other or quoting it in their solo lines. After two minutes, they converge on the riff, guitar joins in, drums return, and there is a new fast tutti unison theme to end.

While the historical narrative implied by "A Jackson in Your House" has free jazz swallowing jazz history by claiming it as its subject and material and accepting a proliferation of practices, the narrative implied by "Dogon A.D." suggests free jazz becoming absorbed into a more expansive concept of jazz history and an expanded common practice. The arrangements and improvisations on the recordings considered approach it from multiple genres and idioms, as well as an object of historical recreation. For these artists, and many others who grew up with free jazz, its innovations are neither the triumphant end of jazz history nor a failed detour, but part of the tradition.

Notes

Introduction

1. Paul Lopes, *The Rise of a Jazz Art World* (New York: Cambridge University Press, 2002).

2. Kenny Mathieson, *Giant Steps: Bebop and the Creators of Modern Jazz, 1945–65* (Edinburgh: Payback, 1999), 194; Paul Bley, with David Lee, *Stopping Time: Paul Bley and the Transformation of Jazz* (Montreal: Véhicule, 1999), 25–26, 56, 61; Norman Meehan, *Time Will Tell: Conversations with Paul Bley* (Albany, CA: Berkeley Hills Books, 2003), 14–15; Gunther Schuller, *Musings: The Musical Worlds of Gunther Schuller* (New York: Oxford University Press, 1986), 18–25.

3. Bill Dixon, *L'Opera: A Collection of Letters, Writings, Musical Scores, Drawings, and Photographs (1967–1986), Volume One* (North Bennington, VT: Metamorphosis Music, 1986), 86–87.

4. Brigid Cohen, "Enigmas of the Third Space: Mingus and Varèse at Greenwich House, 1957," *Journal of the American Musicological Society* 71, no. 1 (2018): 155–211; Ted Gioia, *West Coast Jazz: Modern Jazz in California, 1945–1960* (Berkeley: University of California Press, 1998), 233–34; Andy Hamilton, *Lee Konitz: Conversations on the Improviser's Art* (Ann Arbor: University of Michigan Press, 2007), 209–13; Herbert Hellhund, *Cool Jazz: Grundzüge seiner Entstehung und Entwicklung* (New York: Schott, 1985), 119–30, 140–43; Eunmi Shim, *Lennie Tristano: His Life and Music* (Ann Arbor: University of Michigan Press, 2007), 48–55; David Toop, *Into the Maelstrom: Music, Improvisation, and the Dream of Freedom, before 1970* (New York: Bloomsbury, 2016), 102–5, 108–9, 115–16, 118–22.

5. LeRoi Jones (Amiri Baraka), *Black Music* (New York: Morrow, 1970), 130, 172–76, 180–211.

6. Graham Lock, *Forces in Motion: The Music and Thoughts of Anthony Braxton* (New York: Da Capo, 1988), 124.

7. Lloyd Peterson, *Music and the Creative Spirit: Innovators in Jazz, Improvisation, and the Avant Garde* (Lanham, MD: Rowman and Littlefield, 2006), 62; Benjamin Looker, *Point from Which Creation Begins: The Black Artists' Group of St.*

Louis (St. Louis: Missouri Historical Society Press, 2004), 168; Floris Schuiling, *Animate Structures: The Compositions and Improvisations of the Instant Composers Pool Orchestra* (PhD diss., Cambridge University, 2015), https://www.repository.cam.ac.uk/handle/1810/273767: 57; Anthony Braxton, *Composition Notes*, 5 vols. (Lebanon, NH: Frog Peak Music, 1988), 1:320; Ronald M. Radano, *New Musical Figurations: Anthony Braxton's Cultural Critique* (Chicago: University of Chicago Press, 1993), 208.

8. George Lewis, *A Power Stronger than Itself: The AACM and American Experimental Music* (Chicago: University of Chicago Press, 2008), 98.

9. Lewis, *A Power Stronger than Itself*, xi–xii.

10. Lewis, *A Power Stronger than Itself*, xliii–xliv.

11. Joe Morris, *Perpetual Frontier: The Properties of Free Music* (Stony Creek, CT: Riti, 2012).

12. Ken Vandermark, "Free Jazz, Genre and Style," in *Arcana VIII: Musicians on Music*, ed. John Zorn (New York: Hip's Road, 2017), 323–38.

13. Thomas Owens, *Bebop: The Music and Its Players* (New York: Oxford University Press, 1995).

14. Morris, *Perpetual Frontier*, 7–9; Amiri Baraka and Amina Baraka, *The Music: Reflections on Jazz and Blues* (New York: Morrow, 1987), 332.

15. Ekkehard Jost, *Free Jazz* (New York: Da Capo, 1994); John Litweiler, *The Freedom Principle: Jazz after 1958* (New York: Quill, 1984); Valerie Wilmer, *As Serious as Your Life: The Story of the New Jazz* (London: Serpent's Tail, 1992).

16. Jones, *Black Music*, 172–211; Ekkehard Jost, "The European Jazz Avant-Garde of the Late 1960s and Early 1970s: Where Did Emancipation Lead?," in *Eurojazzland: Jazz and European Sources, Dynamics, and Contexts*, ed. Luca Cerchiari, Laurent Cugny, and Franz Kerschbaumer (Boston: Northeastern University Press, 2012), 275–97.

17. LeRoi Jones (Amiri Baraka), *Blues People: The Negro Experience in White America and the Music That Developed from It* (New York: Morrow, 1963), 228; Jones, *Black Music*, 55, 105, 107.

18. Iain Anderson, *This Is Our Music: Free Jazz, the Sixties, and American Culture* (Philadelphia: University of Pennsylvania Press, 2007), 153–81; Lewis, *A Power Stronger than Itself*, 330–33, 400–404, 415–20; Looker, *Point from Which Creation Begins*, 52–62.

19. Michael Heller, *Loft Jazz: Improvising New York in the 1970s* (Oakland: University of California Press, 2017); Will Hermes, *Love Goes to Buildings on Fire: Five Years in New York That Changed Music Forever* (New York: Faber and Faber, 2011); Looker, *Point from Which Creation Begins*, 69–72.

20. Paul Steinbeck, *Message to Our Folks: The Art Ensemble of Chicago* (Chicago: University of Chicago Press, 2017), 81–92.

21. Looker, *Point from Which Creation Begins*, 145–48.

Chapter 1

1. Darius Brubeck, "1959: The Beginning of Beyond," in *The Cambridge Companion to Jazz*, ed. Mervyn Cooke and David Horn (Cambridge: Cambridge University Press, 2002), 177–201; Fred Kaplan, *1959: The Year Everything Changed* (Hoboken, NJ: Wiley, 2009), 84–93, 198–211.

2. Schuller, *Musings*, 21.

3. Ian Carr, *Miles Davis: The Definitive Biography* (New York: Harper Collins, 1998), 144–52; Miles Davis, *Kind of Blue: Transcribed Score* (Milwaukee: Hal Leonard, 2001); Miles Davis, and Quincy Troupe, *Miles: The Autobiography* (New York: Simon and Schuster, 1989), 225–26, 230, 233–35; Robert Hodson, *Interaction, Improvisation, and Interplay in Jazz* (New York: Routledge, 2007), 144–62; Jost, *Free Jazz*, 20–24; Lewis Porter, *John Coltrane: His Life and Music* (Ann Arbor: University of Michigan Press, 1998), 158–65; Schuller, *Musings*, 21; Keith Waters, *Postbop Jazz in the 1960s: The Compositions of Wayne Shorter, Herbie Hancock, and Chick Corea* (New York: Oxford University Press, 2019), 16.

4. Jost, *Free Jazz* 23–25; Eric Nisenson, *Ascension: John Coltrane and His Quest* (New York: Da Capo, 1993), 72–73; Porter, *John Coltrane*, 145–58.

5. John Schott, "'We Are Revealing a Hand That Will Later Reveal Us': Notes on Form and Harmony in Coltrane's Later Work," in *Arcana: Musicians on Music*, ed. John Zorn (New York: Granary, 2000), 345–66: 346–48, 354–57.

6. Steven Block, "'Bemsha Swing': The Transformation of a Bebop Classic to Free Jazz," *Music Theory Spectrum* 19, no. 2 (1997): 206–31; Jane Martha Reynolds, *Improvisation Analysis of Selected Works of Albert Ayler, Roscoe Mitchell, and Cecil Taylor* (PhD diss., University of Wisconsin, 1993), 108–23; Schuller, *Musings*, 65–75.

7. Bill Evans, Scott LaFaro, Paul Motian, Liam Noble, and Chris Baron, *The Bill Evans Trio, 1959–1961* (Milwaukee: Hal Leonard, 2010); Hodson, *Interaction, Improvisation, and Interplay in Jazz*, 115–44; Peter Pettinger, *Bill Evans: How My Heart Sings* (New Haven, CT: Yale University Press, 1998), 91–96.

8. Jim Hall, liner notes to *Piece for Clarinet and String Orchestra/Mobiles*, by Jimmy Giuffre, Verve, 1961.

9. Earle Brown, *Novara*, musical score (London: Universal Edition, 1979); Toop, *Into the Maelstrom*, 127.

10. David Lee, *The Battle of the Five Spot: Ornette Coleman and the New York Jazz Field* (Toronto: Mercury, 2006), 14–15; John Litweiler, *Ornette Coleman: A Harmolodic Life* (New York: Da Capo, 1994), 75–91; Peter Niklas Wilson, *Ornette Coleman: His Life and Music* (Berkeley, CA: Berkeley Hills Books, 1999), 26–28; Jeremy Yudkin, *The Lenox School of Jazz: A Vital Chapter in the History of American Music and Race Relations* (South Egremont, MA: Farshaw, 2006), 86–94.

11. Eric Charry, "Freedom and Form in Ornette Coleman's Early Atlantic Recordings," *Annual Review of Jazz Studies* 9 (1997): 285–86, 290–91; Jost, *Free Jazz*, 47–48; Martin Williams, liner notes to *The Shape of Jazz to Come*, by Ornette Coleman, Atlantic, 1959.

12. Ornette Coleman, as told to Gary Kramer, liner notes to *Change of the Century*, by Ornette Coleman, Atlantic, 1960; Ornette Coleman, "To Whom It May Concern" *Downbeat*, June 1, 1967, 19; Ornette Coleman, "Ornette Coleman: Harmolodics and the Oldest Language," *Musician: Player and Listener*, May 1978, 8–10; Ornette Coleman, "Something to Think About," in *Free Spirits: Annals of the Insurgent Imagination*, ed. Paul Buhle, Jayne Cortez, Philip Lamntia, et al. (San Francisco: City Lights, 1982), 117–20; Ornette Coleman, "Prime Time for Harmolodics," *Downbeat*, July 1983, 54–55; Ornette Coleman, Pete Welding, Shelly Manne, and Cannonball Adderley, "Round the Empty Foxhole," *Downbeat*, November 2, 1967, 16–17.

13. Litweiler, *Ornette Coleman*, 29–47.

14. Jost, *Free Jazz*, 45; Lee, *The Battle of the Five Spot*, 78–83; A. B. Spellman, *Four Lives in the Bebop Business* (New York: Limelight, 1985), 118.

15. Williams, liner notes to *The Shape of Jazz to Come*; Schuller, *Musings*, 80–81.

16. Daniel Belgrad, *The Culture of Spontaneity: Improvisation and the Arts in Postwar America* (Chicago: University of Chicago Press, 1998).

17. Anderson, *This Is Our Music*, 65–69.

18. Belgrad, *The Culture of Spontaneity*, 237–39; Lee, *The Battle of the Five Spot*, 47–51; Norman Mailer, *Advertisements for Myself* (Cambridge, MA: Harvard University Press, 1992), 337–58; Scott Saul, *Freedom Is, Freedom Ain't: Jazz and the Making of the Sixties* (Cambridge, MA: Harvard University Press, 2003), 63–72.

19. Schuller, *Musings*.

20. Charry, "Freedom and Form," 264, 285–87, 290–91; Michael B. Cogswell, *Melodic Organization in Four Solos by Ornette Coleman* (MM thesis, University of North Texas, 1989), 62–63, https://digital.library.unt.edu/ark:/67531/metadc501207/; Stephen Rush, *Free Jazz, Harmolodics, and Ornette Coleman* (New York: Routledge, 2017), 151–55, 227–30.

21. Gioia, *West Coast Jazz*, 353–54; Nat Hentoff, liner notes to *Something Else!*, by Ornette Coleman, Contemporary, 1958; Nat Hentoff, liner notes to *Tomorrow Is the Question*, by Ornette Coleman, Contemporary, 1959; Jost, *Free Jazz*, 56–58; Wilson, *Ornette Coleman*, 109.

22. Charry, "Freedom and Form," 265, 267–71, 289; Ethan Iverson, "Interview with Charlie Haden," *Do the M@th* (blog), March 2008, https://ethaniverson.com/interviews/interview-with-charlie-haden/.

23. Bley, *Stopping Time*, 58–68.

24. Cogswell, *Melodic Organization*, 47.

25. Charry, "Freedom and Form," 265–69; Cogswell, *Melodic Organization*, 37; Jost, *Free Jazz*, 47–48.

26. Nikki Joanna Stedman, *The Role of the Bass in Pianoless Jazz Ensembles, 1952–2014*, 2 vols. (PhD diss., University of Adelaide, 2016), 1:182–83, 195; 2:354–78, 381–90, 406–9, 414–20, https://digital.library.adelaide.edu.au/dspace/handle/2440/109798.

27. Charry, "Freedom and Form," 270; Hodson, *Interaction, Improvisation, and Interplay in Jazz*, 162–70; Jost, *Free Jazz*, 51–52.

28. Iverson, "Interview with Charlie Haden."

29. Meehan, *Time Will Tell*, 75.

30. Derek Bailey, *Improvisation: Its Nature and Practice in Music* (New York: Da Capo, 1992), 55.

31. Bley, *Stopping Time*, 63.

32. Porter, *John Coltrane*, 146–53, 166, 170, 173, 188; Waters, *Postbop Jazz in the 1960s*, 18.

33. Wilmer, *As Serious as Your Life*, 60.

34. Stedman, *The Role of the Bass*, 1:182–83, 195; 2:354–78, 381–90, 406–9, 414–20.

35. Charry, "Freedom and Form," 265–85; Iverson, "Interview with Charlie Haden"; Jost, *Free Jazz*, 47–48.

36. Coleman, liner notes to *Change of the Century*.

37. Schuller, *Musings*, 57–58.

38. Schuller, *Musings*, 77.

39. Jost, *Free Jazz*, 59–61.

40. Jost, *Free Jazz*, 134.

41. Litweiler, *Ornette Coleman*, 57.

42. Ornette Coleman, liner notes to *Skies of America*, by Ornette Coleman, Columbia Records, 1972.

43. Rush, *Free Jazz*, xi.

44. Coleman, "Ornette Coleman: Harmolodics"; Coleman, "Prime Time for Harmolodics."

45. Litweiler, *Ornette Coleman*, 93–94; Wilson, *Ornette Coleman*, 9.

46. Morris, *Perpetual Frontier*, 90–91; Wilson, *Ornette Coleman*, 75–76, 85–86.

47. Jost, *Free Jazz*, 49–51.

48. Hentoff, liner notes to *Something Else!*.

49. Martin Williams, *The Jazz Tradition*, 2nd rev. ed. (New York: Oxford University Press, 1993), 236.

50. Matt Lavelle, *Ornette Coleman and Harmolodics* (MA thesis, Rutgers University, 2019), 72, https://rucore.libraries.rutgers.edu/rutgers-lib/60549.

51. Howard Mandel, *Jazz Beyond Jazz: Miles, Ornette, Cecil* (New York: Routledge, 2007), 146–47, 180; Herb Nolan, "Jimmy Garrison: Bassist in the Front Line," *Downbeat*, June 6, 1974, 18.

52. Lavelle, *Ornette Coleman and Harmolodics*, 62, 182. I also heard Ken Wessel present this material at a Creative Music Studio workshop May 22, 2013, and in a webcast from the New York Jazz Workshop May 23, 2020.

53. Meehan, *Time Will Tell*, 52–53, 74–80.

54. Robert W. Sabin, *Gary Peacock: Analysis of Progressive Double Bass Improvisation, 1963–1965* (PhD diss., New York University, 2014), 52, 55–58, 140–41, 168–208, 401, 457–61.

55. Ethan Iverson, "Service for Paul Bley," *Do the M@th* (blog), n.d., https://ethaniverson.com/service-for-paul-bley/; Iverson, "Interview with Charlie Haden"; Ben Ratliff, "Listening to CDs with Pat Metheny: An Idealist Reconnects with His Mentors," *New York Times*, February 25, 2005, E1; Sabin, *Gary Peacock*, 168–69, 401.

56. Ingrid Monson, *Freedom Sounds: Civil Rights Call Out to Jazz and Africa* (New York: Oxford University Press, 2007), 287–88, 291.

57. George Russell, *The Lydian Chromatic Concept of Tonal Organization for Improvisation* (New York: Concept, 1959), xx–xxiii.

58. Russell, *The Lydian Chromatic Concept*, xxii.

59. Litweiler, *Ornette Coleman*, 69, 92.

60. Brian Priestley, *Mingus: A Critical Biography* (New York: Da Capo, 1982), 110–11.

61. Litweiler, *Ornette Coleman*, 91; Porter, *John Coltrane*, 203–4.

62. Kwami Coleman, *The "Second Quintet": Miles Davis, the Jazz Avant-Garde, and Change, 1959–1968* (PhD diss., Stanford University, 2014), 33, 66–77; Davis and Troupe, *Miles*, 249–51, 268–69; Sabin, *Gary Peacock*, 79–81; Keith Waters, *The Studio Recordings of the Miles Davis Quintet, 1965–68* (New York: Oxford University Press, 2011), 37–38.

63. Paul Berliner, *Thinking in Jazz: The Infinite Art of Improvisation* (Chicago: University of Chicago Press, 1994), 340.

64. Coleman, *The "Second Quintet,"* 96–107; Bob Gluck, *The Miles Davis Lost Quintet and Other Revolutionary Ensembles* (Chicago: University of Chicago Press, 2016), 119; Garrett Michaelsen, "'Making Anti-Music:' Divergent Interactional Strategies in the Miles Davis Quintet's *The Complete Live at the Plugged Nickel 1965*," *Music Theory Online* 25, no. 3 (2019), https://www.mtosmt.org/issues/mto.19.25.3/mto.19.25.3.michaelsen.html.

65. Waters, *The Studio Recordings*, 126.

66. Coleman, *The "Second Quintet,"* 109, 129, 131–42; Waters, *The Studio Recordings*, 9, 13, 76–81, 142, 146–53, 210–16, 219–36.

67. Gluck, *The Miles Davis Lost Quintet*, 1–33, 51–56, 160–63.

68. Ethan Iverson, "Shades of Jazz (Keith Jarrett, Charlie Haden, Paul Motian, Dewey Redman)," *Do the M@th* (blog), January 2021, https://ethaniverson.com/shades-of-jazz-keith-jarrett-charlie-haden-paul-motian-dewey-redman/.

69. Mervyn Cooke, *Pat Metheny: The ECM Years, 1975–1984* (New York: Oxford University Press, 2017), 59–60, 156, 159, 214–15, 223–29, 268–69.

70. Rush, *Free Jazz*, ix.

71. Ethan Iverson, "Interview with Stanley Crouch," *Do the M@th* (blog), February 2007, https://ethaniverson.com/interviews/interview-with-stanley-crouch/.
72. Nat Hentoff, *Listen to the Stories: Nat Hentoff on Jazz and Country Music* (New York: Harper Collins, 1995): 141–42; Bill Shoemaker, *Jazz in the Seventies: Diverging Streams* (Lanham, MD: Rowman and Littlefield, 2018), 217.
73. Lavelle, *Ornette Coleman and Harmolodics*, 36–37, 39, 43.
74. Coleman et al., "Round the Empty Foxhole."
75. Litweiler, *Ornette Coleman*, 116–18, 120–21; Wilson, *Ornette Coleman*, 50–51.

Chapter 2

1. Ben Ratliff, *Coltrane: The Story of a Sound* (New York: Farrar, Straus and Giroux, 2007), 53.
2. Porter, *John Coltrane*, 180–81.
3. Peter Lavezzoli, *The Dawn of Indian Music in the West* (New York: Continuum, 2007), 277–78; Porter, *John Coltrane*, 181–84.
4. Davis and Troupe, *Miles*, 225–26, 234–35.
5. Porter, *John Coltrane*, 211–12.
6. Porter, *John Coltrane*, 218.
7. Porter, *John Coltrane*, 209–11.
8. Robin D. G. Kelley, *Africa Speaks, America Answers: Modern Jazz in Revolutionary Times* (Cambridge, MA: Harvard University Press, 2012), 91–119.
9. Lynette Westendorf, *Analyzing Free Jazz* (DMA diss., University of Washington, 1994), 84–86, 119.
10. Carl Clements, "John Coltrane and the Integration of Indian Concepts in Jazz Improvisation," *Jazz Research Journal* 2, no. 2 (2008): 160; Jost, *Free Jazz*, 28–30; Lavezzoli, *The Dawn of Indian Music in the West*, 279–80.
11. Waters, *Postbop Jazz in the 1960s*, 15–17.
12. Anderson, *This Is Our Music*, 110; Lavezzoli, *The Dawn of Indian Music in the West*, 281–89.
13. Franya Berkman, *Monument Eternal: The Music of Alice Coltrane* (Middletown, CT: Wesleyan University Press, 2010), 52; Lavezzoli, *The Dawn of Indian Music in the West*, 280–81.
14. Steven Isoardi, *The Dark Tree: Jazz and the Community Arts in Los Angeles* (Berkeley: University of California Press, 2006), 297.
15. Porter, *John Coltrane*, 206–8.
16. Anthony Brown, "John Coltrane as the Personification of Spirituality in Black Music," in *John Coltrane and Black America's Quest for Freedom: Spirituality and the Music*, ed. Leonard L. Brown (New York: Oxford University Press, 2010), 58.

17. Conversation with the author, probably November 2015.

18. Jason C. Bivins, *Spirits Rejoice! Jazz and American Religion* (New York: Oxford University Press, 2015), 136; Ratliff, *Coltrane*, 71.

19. Bivins, *Spirits Rejoice!*, 136; Ashley Kahn, *A Love Supreme: The Story of John Coltrane's Signature Album* (New York: Viking, 2002), 79.

20. Saul, *Freedom Is, Freedom Ain't*, 239–43.

21. Bivins, *Spirits Rejoice!*, 137.

22. Anderson, *This Is Our Music*, 115; Ashley Kahn, *The House That Trane Built: The Story of Impulse Records* (New York: Norton, 2006), 119.

23. Bivins, *Spirits Rejoice!*, 30.

24. Bivins, *Spirits Rejoice!*, 98–99, 157–64; Kimberly Hannon Teal, *Jazz Places: How Performance Spaces Shape Jazz History* (Berkeley: University of California Press, 2021), 71–73.

25. John Coltrane, *A Love Supreme: Acknowledgement, Resolution, Pursuance, Psalm* (Milwaukee: Hal Leonard, 2003); Porter, *John Coltrane*, 232–49.

26. Porter, *John Coltrane*, 242–43.

27. Kahn, *A Love Supreme*, 103; David Liebman, "John Coltrane's *Meditations* Suite: A Study in Symmetry," *Annual Review of Jazz Studies* 8 (1996): 169–74; Marc Medwin, "Attaining Unity: Self-Reference in the Music of John Coltrane," *Jazz Research Journal* 2, no. 2 (2009): 119–31.

28. Porter, *John Coltrane*, 244–48.

29. Ratliff, *Coltrane*, 102.

30. Lavezzoli, *The Dawn of Indian Music in the West*, 285.

31. Bivins, *Spirits Rejoice!*, 137–38; Porter, *John Coltrane*, 264–66; Ratliff, *Coltrane*, 168.

32. Kahn, *The House That Trane Built*, 179.

33. Berkman, *Monument Eternal*, 7, 53, 68–69.

34. Berkman, *Monument Eternal*, 53; Bivins, *Spirits Rejoice!*, 143–44; Porter, *John Coltrane*, 211.

35. Berkman, *Monument Eternal*, 82–90.

36. Berkman, *Monument Eternal*, 57.

37. William Sites, *Sun Ra's Chicago: Afrofuturism and the City* (Chicago: University of Chicago Press, 2020), 179–99; John Szwed, *Space is the Place: The Lives and Times of Sun Ra*, 2nd ed. (Durham, NC: Duke University Press, 2020), 150-151; David Toop, *Exotica: Fabricated Soundscapes in a Real World* (London: Serpent's Tail), 1999, 39–41.

38. Sites, *Sun Ra's Chicago*, 112–18.

39. Alice Coltrane, liner notes to *Journey in Satchidananda*, by Alice Coltrane, Impulse, 1971.

40. Babatunde Olatunji, with Robert Atkinson, assisted by Akinsola Akiwono, forward by Joan Baez, introduction by Eric Charry, *The Beat of My Drum: An Autobiography* (Philadelphia: Temple University Press, 2005), 2–3, 94–96, 117–18, 130–52.

41. Olatunji, *The Beat of My Drum*, 152.
42. Olatunji, *The Beat of My Drum*, 147.
43. Olatunji, *The Beat of My Drum*, 5–7.
44. Kelley, *Africa Speaks, America Answers*, 32–34; Olatunji, *The Beat of My Drum*, 4, 11–12.
45. Kelley, *Africa Speaks, America Answers*, 56–64; Monson, *Freedom Sounds*, 147–51, 171–81; Olatunji, *The Beat of My Drum*, 7–8.
46. Berkman, *Monument Eternal*, 52; Carter Mathes, *Imagine the Sound: Experimental African-American Literature after Civil Rights* (Minneapolis: University of Minnesota Press, 2015), 27–31.
47. Szwed, *Space Is the Place*, 202–3.
48. On jazz and Negritude, see Tsitsi Ella Jaji, *Africa in Stereo: Modernism, Music, and Pan-African Solidarity* (New York: Oxford University Press, 2014), 66–110.
49. Robert R. MacLean, *After Modern Jazz: The Avant-Garde and Jazz Historiography* (PhD diss., University of Michigan, 2011), 276, 283–91, https://deepblue.lib.umich.edu/handle/2027.42/89753; Elaine Mokhtefi, *Algiers, Third World Capital: Freedom Fighters, Revolutionaries, Black Panthers* (London: Verso, 2018), 92–94; Celeste Day Moore, *Soundscapes of Liberation: African American Music in Postwar France* (Durham, NC: Duke University Press, 2021), 181–87.
50. MacLean, *After Modern Jazz*, 293.
51. Kahn, *The House That Trane Built*, 201.
52. Kahn, *A Love Supreme*, 166.
53. Jones, *Black Music*, 123; Frank Kofsky, *Black Nationalism and the Revolution in Music* (New York: Pathfinder, 1970), 147.
54. Mathes, *Imagine the Sound*, 29–30.
55. Bivins, *Spirits Rejoice!*, 142–45; Lavezzoli, *The Dawn of Indian Music in the West*, 290; Mark McNeill, *Forevermore Transcending: The Ashram Albums of Alice "Swamini Turiyasangitananda" Coltrane* (MA thesis, University of Southern California, 2016).
56. Peter Jan Margry and Daniel Wojcik "A Saxophone Divine: Experiencing the Transformative Power of Saint John Coltrane's Jazz Music in San Francisco's Fillmore District," in *Spiritualizing the City: Agency and Resilience of the Urban and Urbanesque Habitat*, ed. Victoria Hegner and Peter Jan Margry (New York: Routledge, 2017), 177–78.
57. Nicholas Louis Baham III, *The Coltrane Church: Apostles of Sound, Agents of Social Justice* (Jefferson, NC: McFarland, 2015); Bivins, *Spirits Rejoice!*, 139–42.
58. Michael Coyle, "Pops, Pygmies, and Pentecostal Fire: Sanders and Thomas's 'The Creator Has a Master Plan,'" in *Black Music, Black Poetry: Blues and Jazz's Impact on African American Versification*, ed. Gordon E. Thompson (Burlington, VT: Ashgate, 2013), 178–79.
59. Gabriel Solis, "Timbral Virtuosity: Pharoah Sanders, Sonic Heterogeneity, and the Jazz Avant-Garde in the 1960s and 70s," *Jazz Perspectives* 9, no. 1 (2015): 54–55.

60. Jones, *Black Music*, 210–11; Solis, "Timbral Virtuosity," 61–63.

61. Matthew B. Karush, "Reinventing the Latin in Latin Jazz: The Music and Career of Gato Barbieri," *Journal of Latin American Cultural Studies* 25, no. 3 (2016): 386–87.

62. Greg Tate, *Flyboy in the Buttermilk: Essays on Contemporary America* (New York: Simon and Schuster, 1992), 73–82.

63. Amiri Baraka, *The Autobiography of LeRoi Jones* (Chicago: Lawrence Hill, 1997), 350–51, 355–60, 383, 385–93, 403–8.

64. Scot Brown, *Fighting for US: Maulana Karenga, the US Organization, and Black Cultural Nationalism* (New York: New York University Press, 2003), 138–42.

65. Solis, "Timbral Virtuosity," 63–65.

66. Isoardi, *The Dark Tree*, 120–21.

67. Isoardi, *The Dark Tree*, 128.

68. Isoardi, *The Dark Tree*, 256–58, 298, 300.

69. Isoardi, *The Dark Tree*, 105–107, 122–127; Horace Tapscott, *Songs of the Unsung: The Musical and Social Journey of Horace Tapscott*, ed. Steven Isoardi (Durham, NC: Duke University Press, 2001), 112–13, 122–24.

70. Hermes, *Love Goes to Buildings on Fire*, 163–64.

Chapter 3

1. Christopher G. Bakriges, *African American Musical Avant-Gardism* (PhD diss., York University, 2001), 42.

2. A. B. Spellman, liner notes to *Ascension*, by John Coltrane, Impulse, 1965; Jones, *Black Music*, 193.

3. Lawrence P. Neal [as Laurence], untitled, *Negro Digest*, January 1968, 81.

4. Jones, *Black Music*, 174.

5. David G. Such, *Avant-Garde Jazz Musicians: Performing "Out There"* (Iowa City: University of Iowa Press, 1993), 29.

6. Steven Heffner, *An Analysis of Dave Holland's Free Improvisation "Waterfall" and Its Pedagogical Implications for Bassists in Avant-Garde Performance* (DMA diss., University of North Texas, 2019), 5, 41–51, https://digital.library.unt.edu/ark:/67531/metadc1609128/; Jost, *Free Jazz*, 126–27; Reynolds, *Improvisation Analysis*, 111–12, 132, 212.

7. Reynolds, *Improvisation Analysis*, 111–12, 132, 212.

8. Conversation with the author at the Vancouver Creative Music Institute, June 2008.

9. Sabin, *Gary Peacock*, 248–52.

10. Jost, *Free Jazz*, 69–72.

11. Dan Warburton, "Sunny Murray," *Paris Transatlantic*, November 3, 2000, http://www.paristransatlantic.com/magazine/interviews/murray.html; Spellman, *Four Lives in the Bebop Business*, 45; Wilmer, *As Serious as Your Life*, 160.

12. Spellman, *Four Lives in the Bebop Business*, 75.
13. John Sinclair, and Robert Levin, *Music and Politics* (New York: World Publishing, 1971), 73.
14. Bley, *Stopping Time*, 86.
15. Bley, *Stopping Time*, 89–90.
16. Jones, *Black Music*, 116, 127.
17. Graham Lock, *Chasing the Vibration: Meetings with Creative Musicians* (Devon: Stride, 1994), 123; Warburton, "Sunny Murray."
18. James Gordon Williams, *Crossing Bar Lines: The Politics and Practices of Black Musical Space* (Jackson: University Press of Mississippi, 2021), 56–69.
19. Jones, *Black Music*, 134.
20. Sabin, *Gary Peacock*, 65–66, 417.
21. Jones, *Black Music*, 126.
22. Paul Hegarty, *Noise/Music: A History* (New York: Continuum, 2007), 47.
23. Kasper Collin, dir., *My Name Is Albert Ayler* (Luleå, Sweden: Filmpool Nord, 2006).
24. Lock, *Forces in Motion*, 186–87; William Parker, *Conversations* (Paris: Rogueart, 2011), 263.
25. Parker, *Conversations*, 263–64.
26. Mathes, *Imagine the Sound*, 32–34.
27. Jones, *Black Music*, 193–94.
28. Amiri Baraka, "Malcolm as Ideology," in *Malcolm X: In Our Own Image*, ed. Joe Wood (New York: Anchor, 1994), 18–35; Amiri Baraka, "Confessions of a Former Anti-Semite," *Village Voice*, December 17–23, 1980, 20; St. Clair Bourne, "An Interview with Allen Ginsberg," in *Amiri Baraka: The Kalidescopic Torch*, ed. James B. Gwynne (New York: Steppingstones, 1985), 78.
29. Ben Young and Carlos Kase, "Sightings," in *Holy Ghost: Rare and Unissued Recordings (1962–1970)*, by Albert Ayler, Revenant Records, 2004, 200; "For the Benefit of the Black Arts: Improvisation, Jazz, Dancing, Party," advertisement, *Village Voice*, February 25, 1965, 8; K. Komozi Woodard and Randolph H. Boehm, eds., *The Black Power Movement, Part 1: Amiri Baraka from Black Arts to Black Radicalism* (Bethesda, MD: University Publications of America, 2001).
30. "School and Theater Planned in Harlem by LeRoi Jones," *New York Times*, February 23, 1965, 40.
31. "Arms Cache and 6 Seized in Harlem," *New York Times*, March 17, 1966, 30; Baraka, *The Autobiography of LeRoi Jones*, 328–30; Michael Oren, "A '60s Saga: The Life and Death of Umbra, Part II," *Freedomways* 24, no. 4 (1984): 250; Michael Stern, "Arms Cache Laid to Small Group: But Harlem Racists Aimed for Power, Police Say," *New York Times*, March 19, 1966, 27; Michael Stern, "Police Look into Harlem Racists: Arms Cache Found in Raid on Black Arts Theater," *New York Times*, March 18, 1966, 18; K. Komozi Woodard, *The Making of the New Ark: Imamu Amiri Baraka (LeRoi Jones), the Newark Congress of African People, and the Modern Black Convention Movement: A History of the*

Black Revolt and the New Nationalism, 1966–1976 (PhD diss., University of Pennsylvania, 1991), 62–63.

32. Monson, *Freedom Sounds*, 157–60.

33. William J. Harris, "Amiri Baraka among the Bohemians: 27 Cooper Square," in *Some Other Blues: New Perspectives on Amiri Baraka*, ed. Jean-Philippe Marcoux (Columbus, OH: Ohio State University Press, 2021), 15–22.

34. Hettie Jones, *How I Became Hettie Jones* (New York: Dutton, 1990), 169–72; Larry Nai, "Marzette Watts Interview," *Cadence* 24, no. 8 (1998): 13–15; Claudia Moreno Pisano, ed., *Amiri Baraka and Edward Dorn: The Collected Letters* (Albuquerque: University of New Mexico Press, 2013), 88, 130; Gilbert Sorrentino, "*Neon, Kulchur*, etc.," in *The Little Magazine in America: A Modern Documentary History*, ed. Elliott Anderson and Mary Kinzie (Yonkers, NY: Pushcart, 1978), 307; Such, *Avant-Garde Jazz Musicians*, 26.

35. Bernard Gendron, "After the October Revolution: The Jazz Avant-Garde in New York, 1964–65," in *Sound Commitments: Avant-Garde Music and the Sixties*, ed. Robert Adlington (New York: Oxford University Press, 2009), 215.

36. Kofsky, *Black Nationalism and the Revolution in Music*, 131–32.

37. Kahn, *The House That Trane Built*, 132; Such, *Avant-Garde Jazz Musicians*, 71.

38. Brown, *John Coltrane and Black America's Quest*, 60.

39. Norman C. Weinstein, *A Night in Tunisia: Imaginings of Africa in Jazz* (New York: Limelight, 1992), 68.

40. Jost, *Free Jazz*, 89–90, 94; Spellman, liner notes to *Ascension*; Westendorf, *Analyzing Free Jazz*, 9.

41. Spellman, liner notes to *Ascension*; Jones, *Black Music*, 195.

42. Spellman, liner notes to *Ascension*.

43. Hegarty, *Noise/Music*, 48–49.

44. Szwed, *Space Is the Place*, 259–60.

45. Szwed, *Space Is the Place*, 99.

46. Wilmer *As Serious as Your Life*, 95.

47. Paul Rinzler, *The Contradictions of Jazz* (Lanham, MD: Scarecrow, 2008), 17–37, 101–9.

48. Jones, *Black Music*, 176.

49. Keith Waters, "'New Awakenings Everywhere: Free Jazz Pathways Through Western Europe' by Ekkehard Jost," *Jazz Perspectives* 10, no. 2–3 (2017): 166.

50. Peter Brötzmann, *We Thought We Could Change the World: Conversations with Gérard Rouy* (Hofheim, Germany: Wolke, 2014), 92; Mike Heffley, *Northern Sun, Southern Moon: Europe's Reinvention of Jazz* (New Haven, CT: Yale University Press, 2005), 329.

51. Waters, "New Awakenings Everywhere," 163.

52. Jost, "The European Jazz Avant-Garde of the Late 1960s and Early 1970s," 281–83; Waters, "New Awakenings Everywhere," 166–68.
53. Shoemaker, *Jazz in the Seventies*, 52.
54. Steven A. Loewy, "Peter Brötzmann: Leader of the Pack Unmasked," *Coda*, March/April 1999, 10.
55. Brötzmann, *We Thought*, 13–17.
56. Harald Kisiedu, *European Echoes: Jazz Experimentalism in Germany, 1950–1975* (Hofheim, Germany: Wolke, 2020), 45–47.
57. Heffley, *Northern Sun, Southern Moon*, 19, 119, 133.
58. Kisiedu, *European Echoes*, 48–64.
59. Jost, "The European Jazz Avant-Garde of the Late 1960s and Early 1970s," 276–77.
60. Heffley, *Northern Sun, Southern Moon*, 99.
61. Heffley, *Northern Sun, Southern Moon*, 101–102.
62. Heffley, *Northern Sun, Southern Moon*, 126–27; Jost, "The European Jazz Avant-Garde of the Late 1960s and Early 1970s," 277–81.
63. George E. Lewis, "*Gittin' to Know Y'All:* Improvised Music, Interculturalism and the Racial Imagination," *Critical Studies in Improvisation* 1, no. 1 (2004): 18–19, https://www.criticalimprov.com/index.php/csieci/article/view/6.
64. Brötzmann, *We Thought*, 90.
65. Toop, *Into the Maelstrom*, 235.
66. John Wickes, *Innovations in British Jazz*, vol. 1, *1960–1980* (Chelmsford, UK: Soundworld, 1999), 249.
67. Kisiedu, *European Echoes*, 9–11; Lewis, "*Gittin' to Know Y'All*," 3–4.
68. Brötzmann, *We Thought*, 41–42.
69. Brötzmann, *We Thought*, 90; Kisiedu, *European Echoes*, 221.
70. Kisiedu, *European Echoes*, 65–66.
71. Brötzmann, *We Thought*, 46.
72. Kisiedu, *European Echoes*, 25.
73. Kisiedu, *European Echoes*, 31–33.
74. Brötzmann, *We Thought*, 23.
75. Toop, *Into the Maelstrom*, 297.
76. Kisiedu, *European Echoes*, 27–28; Waters, "New Awakenings Everywhere," 162–63.
77. Parker, *Conversations*, 410–12.
78. Wolfram Knauer, "1968—Bremen—Brötzmann: Eine Reflektion über das ungewollt Revolutionäre eines Jazzalbums," in *Jazzforschung heute Themen, Methoden, Perspektiven*, ed. Martin Pfeiderer and Wolf-George Zaddach (Berlin: Edition Emvass, 2019), 83–85, 87, 89–90; Hank Shteamer, "Raging against the Machine: Another Look at Peter Brötzmann's *Machine Gun*," *Dark Forces Swing Blind Punches* (blog), March 20, 2011, https://darkforcesswing.blogspot.com/2011/03/raging-against-machine-another-look-at.html.

79. Thurston Moore, "Top Ten from the Free Jazz Underground," *Grand Royal* 2 (1995): 29.
80. Patrick Burke, *Tear Down the Walls: White Radicalism and Black Power in 1960s Rock* (Chicago: University of Chicago Press, 2021), 21–37.
81. Soejima Teruto, *Free Jazz in Japan: A Personal History*, trans. Kato David Hopkins (Nara, Japan: Public Bath, 2018), 12–13.
82. E. Taylor Atkins, *Blue Nippon: Authenticating Jazz in Japan* (Durham, NC: Duke University Press, 2001), 217–33.
83. Teruto, *Free Jazz in Japan*, 35–37.
84. Atkins, *Blue Nippon*, 241–59.
85. Teruto, *Free Jazz in Japan*, 41–43.
86. Teruto, *Free Jazz in Japan*, 66–68.

Chapter 4

1. Shoemaker, *Jazz in the Seventies*, 137–139.
2. Lock, *Chasing the Vibration*, 116.
3. David Borgo, *Sync or Swarm: Improvising Music in a Complex Age* (New York: Continuum, 2005), 75–82; Heffner, *An Analysis*, 12–16, 22–29, 35–37, 39–40.
4. Waters, "New Awakenings Everywhere," 171.
5. Simon H. Fell, *A More Attractive "Way of Getting Things Done": Freedom, Collaboration, and Compositional Paradox in British Improvised Music, 1965–75* (PhD diss., University of Huddersfield, 2017), 65–66, 79–82, http://eprints.hud.ac.uk/id/eprint/34533/.
6. Brian Olewnick, *Keith Rowe: The Room Extended* (Brooklyn, NY: Powerhouse, 2018), 70–82; Edwin Prévost, *No Sound Is Innocent: AMM and the Practice of Musical Self-invention, Meta-musical Narratives, Essays* (Harlow, UK: Copula, 1995), 1, 10–12, 52–54, 61–63, and passim; Ben Watson, *Derek Bailey and the Story of Free Improvisation* (London: Verso, 2004), 60–61, 110–11, 117, 225.
7. Andrew E. Callingham, *Spontaneous Music: The First Generation British Free Improvisers* (PhD diss., University of Huddersfield, 2007), 243, http://eprints.hud.ac.uk/id/eprint/4659; Waters, "New Awakenings Everywhere," 170.
8. Hugh Davies, *Sounds Heard: A Potpourri of Environmental Projects and Documentation, Projects with Children, Simple Musical Instruments, Sound Installations, Verbal Scores, and Historical Perspectives* (Chelmsford, UK: Soundworld, 2002), 27–29.
9. Callingham, *Spontaneous Music*, 43–46.
10. Dan Warburton, "Evan Parker," *Paris Transatlantic*, January 30, 2010, http://paristransatlantic.com/magazine/interviews/parker.html.
11. Waters, "New Awakenings Everywhere," 170.

12. Warburton, "Evan Parker."
13. Nat Hentoff, "The Persistent Challenge of Cecil Taylor," *Downbeat*, February 25, 1965, 17.
14. Valerie Wilmer, *Jazz People* (Indianapolis: Bobbs-Merrill, 1970), 28.
15. Mark J. Bobak, *The Music of Cecil Taylor: An Analysis of Selected Piano Solos 1973–89* (D.M.A. dissertation. University of Illinois at Urbana-Champaign, 1994), 276–77; Jost, *Free Jazz*, 78–83; Mark Peter Wyatt Lockett, *Improvising Pianists: Aspects of Keyboard Technique and Musical Structure in Free Jazz, 1955–1980* (PhD diss., City University London, 1988), 124–30, http://openaccess.city.ac.uk/8259/; Cecil Taylor, "Sound Structure of Subculture Becoming Major Breath/Naked Fire Gesture," liner notes for *Unit Structures*, by Cecil Taylor, Blue Note, 1966.
16. Bobak, *The Music of Cecil Taylor*, 44–55; Morris, *Perpetual Frontier*, 79–82.
17. Morris, *Perpetual Frontier*, 82, 85.
18. Spellman, *Four Lives in the Bebop Business*, 44.
19. Whitney Balliett, *American Musicians II: Seventy-One Portraits in Jazz* (New York: Oxford University Press, 1985), 520.
20. Matthew Kiroff, *"Caseworks" as Performed by Cecil Taylor and the Art Ensemble of Chicago: A Musical Analysis and Sociopolitical History* (DMA diss. Cornell University, 1997), 79, 81, 140–41.
21. Matthew Goodheart, *Freedom and Individuality in the Music of Cecil Taylor* (MA thesis, Mills College, 1996), 40, http://www.matthewgoodheart.com/TaylorThesis/Cecil_Taylor_Thesis-Goodheart.pdf.
22. Shoemaker, *Jazz in the Seventies*, 187.
23. Larry Nai, "Sam Rivers" *Cadence*, October 1999, 5–12, 137. This was also my experience playing Taylor's music in an ensemble led by Karen Borca and including several other Taylor alumni at Brooklyn College, October 26, 2019.
24. Bobak 1994; Lockett, *Improvising Pianists*, 130–34.
25. Mark Miller, "Cecil Taylor: Musician, Poet, Dancer," *Coda*, June/July 1988, 5.
26. Bivins, *Spirits Rejoice!*, 184–90; J. B. Figi, "Cecil Taylor: African Code, Black Methodology," *Downbeat*, April 10, 1975, 31.
27. Gluck, *The Miles Davis Lost Quintet*, 60–62, 75–78.
28. Lewis, *A Power Stronger than Itself*, 96–125.
29. Leo Smith, *Notes (8 Pieces) Source a New World Music: Creative Music* (Chicago: Corbett vs. Dempsey, 2015).
30. Gregory Allen Campbell, *"A Beautiful, Shining Sound Object": Contextualizing Multi-instrumentalism in the Association for the Advancement of Creative Musicians* (DMA diss., University of Washington, 2006), 319–20.
31. Smith, *Notes*.
32. Bill Milkowski, "Wadada Leo Smith's Ankhrasmation Symbolic Language Art-Scores," *Downbeat*, August 2019, 90–93; Hamza Walker, "Ankhras-

mation: Wadada Leo Smith's Language Scores," in *Made in L.A. 2016: A, The, Though, Only*, ed. Aram Moshayedi and Hamza Walker (Los Angeles: Hammer Museum, 2016), 237, 242–43.

33. Smith, *Notes*.

34. Walker, "Ankhrasmation," 240.

35. Milkowski, "Wadada Leo Smith's," 91–93; Walker, "Ankhrasmation," 236–37, 240, 245.

36. Bley, *Stopping Time*, 58–68.

37. Anthony Braxton, *Tri-Axium Writings*, 3 vols. (Lebanon, NH: Synthesis Music, 1985); Anthony Braxton, *Composition Notes*, 5 vols. (Lebanon, NH: Synthesis Music, 1988).

38. Braxton, *Composition Notes*, 1:xi–xviii; 3:600–602, 633–37; 4:504–5; Lock, *Forces in Motion*, 10–11, 216–21.

39. Braxton, *Composition Notes*, 1:29.

40. Braxton, *Composition Notes*, 1:47–50.

41. Gluck, *The Miles Davis Lost Quintet*, 184–87.

42. Braxton, *Composition Notes*, 1:173–83; Radano, *New Musical Figurations*, 122.

43. Braxton, *Composition Notes*, 1:253–62; Anthony Braxton, "8KN-(J-6)-R10" [Composition 18], in *Source: Music of the Avant-Grade, 1966–1973*, ed. Larry Austin and Douglas Kahn (Berkeley: University of California Press, 2011), 320–26.

44. Braxton, *Composition Notes*, 2:34–38.

45. Lock, *Forces in Motion*, 274; Gluck, *The Miles Davis Lost Quintet*, 70–75.

46. Frederic Rzewski, "Les Moutons de Panurge," 1969, https://imslp.org/wiki/Les_Moutons_de_Panurge_(Rzewski%2C_Frederic).

47. Braxton, *Composition Notes*, 3:340–55; Anthony Braxton, *Composition No. 58 for Creative Marching Orchestra (1976)* (Brooklyn, NY: Tri-Centric Foundation, 2015).

48. Braxton, *Composition Notes*, 3:356–66; Anthony Braxton, *Composition No. 59 for Two Soloists and Twelve Instrumentalists (1976)* (Brooklyn, NY: Tri-Centric Foundation, 2015).

49. Braxton, *Composition Notes*, 4:136–54.

50. Paul Steinbeck, "Improvisation and Collaboration in Anthony Braxton's Composition 76," *Journal of Music Theory* 62, no. 2 (2018): 256.

51. Braxton, *Composition Notes*, 5:399–408; Anthony Braxton, *Composition 76 for Three Musicians (1977)* (Brooklyn, NY: Tri-Centric Foundation, 2014).

52. Braxton, *Composition Notes*, 5:411–22; Anthony Braxton, *Composition 115 for Any Instrumentation (1984)* (Brooklyn, NY: Tri-Centric Foundation, 2018).

53. Lock, *Forces in Motion*, 51.

54. Braxton, *Composition Notes*, 1:v–x; Lock, *Forces in Motion*, 27–28, 50–51, 167.

55. Braxton, *Composition Notes*, 1:118–66; 2:194–223; 4:158–246; 5:62–75, 89–116, 259–84, 334–49, 445–92; Lock, *Forces in Motion*, 321.

56. Braxton, *Composition Notes*, 4:229–30.

57. Sean Sonderegger, *"It's More Personal than We Think": Conducted Improvisation Systems and Community in NYC* (MA thesis, Wesleyan University, 2014), 40–50, https://digitalcollections.wesleyan.edu/object/ir-2548; Katherine Young, "Anthony Braxton's Trillium Opera Complex," *Sound American*, no. 16 (2016), http://archive.soundamerican.org/sa_archive/sa16/sa16-the-trillium-operas.html.

58. Braxton, *Composition Notes*, 5:302–33; Anthony Braxton, *Composition 108: Four Pulse Track Structures, for Any Instrumentation (1984)* (Brooklyn, NY: Tri-Centric Foundation, 2018); Lock, *Forces in Motion*, 60, 121, 195–98; Radano, *New Musical Figurations*, 201–2.

59. Lock, *Forces in Motion*, 30, 60, 76, 110–11, 146, 159, 174, 176–77.

60. Braxton, *Composition Notes*, 1:392–404.

61. Erika Dicker, "Ghost Trance Music," *Sound American*, no. 16 (2016), http://archive.soundamerican.org/sa_archive/sa16/sa16-ghost-trance-music.html.

62. Kyoko Kitamura and Anne Rhodes, "Syntactical Ghost Trance Music: A Conversation," *Sound American*, no. 16 (2016), http://archive.soundamerican.org/sa_archive/sa16/sa16-syntactical-ghost-trance-music.html.

63. Taylor Ho Bynum, introduction, liner notes to Anthony Braxton, *9 Compositions (Iridium) 2006*, Firehouse 12 Records, 2007.

64. I performed in the Vancouver Sonic Genome.

65. Carl Testa, "Echo Echo Mirror House Music," *Sound American*, no. 16 (2016), http://archive.soundamerican.org/sa_archive/sa16/sa16-echo-echo-mirror-house-music.html.

66. Rachel Bernsen, "Pine Top Aerial Music" *Sound American*, no. 16 (2016), http://archive.soundamerican.org/sa_archive/sa16/sa16-pine-top-aerial-music.html; Firehouse 12 Records, webpage for *12 Comp (ZIM) 2017*, by Anthony Braxton, https://firehouse12records.com/album/12-comp-zim-2017; Kitamura and Rhodes, "Syntactical Ghost Trance Music."

67. Chad E. Taylor, *Henry Threadgill's Zooid: An Examination of Form and Process* (MA thesis, Rutgers University, 2015), 20, 22, https://rucore.libraries.rutgers.edu/rutgers-lib/47713/.

68. Taylor, *Henry Threadgill's Zooid*, 32–56.

69. Taylor, *Henry Threadgill's Zooid*, 30–32.

70. Threadgill discussed Carter at a Creative Music Studio workshop on June 11, 2014 and in a lecture at UCLA on April 16, 2019, both of which I attended; Lewis, *A Power Stronger than Itself*, 177.

71. Taylor, *Henry Threadgill's Zooid*, 145.

72. Taylor, *Henry Threadgill's Zooid*, 154.

73. Taylor, *Henry Threadgill's Zooid*, 66–69.

74. Taylor, *Henry Threadgill's Zooid*, 112–13, 117.

75. Taylor, *Henry Threadgill's Zooid*, 57–65, 89–91, 148–49, 159.

76. Jeffrey Arlo Brown, "Malleable Structures: An Interview with Tyshawn Sorey," *Van Magazine*, Novmeber 9, 2017, https://van-magazine.com/mag/

tyshawn-sorey/; Kate Gentile, "Peripheral Dromes: Unfamiliar Earworms," in *Arcana IX: Musicians on Music*, ed. John Zorn (New York: Hips Road, 2021), 165.

77. Jost, *Free Jazz*, 187; Szwed, *Space Is the Place*, 212–14.

78. Lawrence "Butch" Morris, *The Art of Conduction: A Conduction Workbook* (New York: Karma, 2017), 14, 185; William Parker, *Conversations II: Dialogues and Monologues* (Paris: Rogueart, 2015), 73, 77; Sonderegger, "It's More Personal than We Think," 62–64; Thomas T. Stanley, *Butch Morris and the Art of Conduction* (PhD diss. University of Maryland, 2009), 50–51, https://drum.lib.umd.edu/handle/1903/9935; Tapscott, *Songs of the Unsung*, 101.

79. Lawrence "Butch" Morris, liner notes to *Testament: A Conduction Collection*, by Lawrence "Butch" Morris, New World Records, 1995, 2, www.newworldrecords.org/liner_notes/80478.pdf.

80. Morris, *The Art of Conduction*, 2–3.

81. Morris, *The Art of Conduction*, 34–35.

82. Sonderegger, "It's More Personal than We Think," 59, 71–72.

83. Morris, *The Art of Conduction*, 187.

84. Morris, *The Art of Conduction*, 83.

85. Morris, *The Art of Conduction*, 29, 160; Walter Thompson, *Soundpainting: The Art of Live Composition, Workbook I* (New York: self-pub., 2006), 2–4.

86. Sonderegger, "It's More Personal than We Think," 88–98. Also, I performed with Rudolph in Los Angeles in October 2013, February 2015, and March 2016.

87. Adam Rudolph, *Pure Rhythm: Rhythm Cycles and Polymetric Patterns for Instrumentalists, Percussionists, Composers and Music Educators* (Rottenburg, Germany: Advance Music, 2005).

88. Dylan van der Schyff, "The Free Improvisation Game: Performing John Zorn's *Cobra*," *Journal of Research in Music Performance*, Spring 2013, 2–3, https://scholar.lib.vt.edu/ejournals/JRMP/2013/schyff.pdf.

89. Bill Shoemaker, "Page One," *Point of Departure*, no. 67 (2019), https://pointofdeparture.org/archives/PoD-67/PoD67PageOne.html.

90. van der Schyff, "The Free Improvisation Game," 7–8.

91. Bailey, *Improvisation*, 75–76.

92. van der Schyff, "The Free Improvisation Game," 4–5.

93. Cisco Bradley, *Universal Tonality: The Life and Music of William Parker* (Durham, NC: Duke University Press, 2021), 196–99, 211.

94. Larry Ochs, "RADAR and ROVA's Development of Language for Structured Improvisation," *ROVA: Arts*, 1999, https://www.rova.org/foodforthought/radar.html.

95. Richard Scott, *Noises: Free Music, Improvisation, and the Avant-Garde: London 1965 to 1990* (PhD diss., London School of Economics, 1991), 53, http://etheses.lse.ac.uk/1134/.

96. Wickes, *Innovations in British Jazz*, 56.

97. Lock, *Chasing the Vibration*, 166.

98. Bailey, *Improvisation*, 118–122; Wickes, *Innovations in British Jazz*, 103.

99. John Stevens, Julia Doyle, and Ollie Crook, *Search and Reflect: Concepts and Pieces by John Stevens* (London: Community Music, 1985).
100. Pete Moser, and George McKay, eds., *Community Music: A Handbook* (Lyme Regis, UK: Russell House, 2005); Community Music, "About Community Music," https://www.cmsounds.com/about.
101. Wickes, *Innovations in British Jazz*, 57–58.
102. Martin Davidson, liner notes to *For You to Share*, by Spontaneous Music Orchestra, Emanem, 1998; Stevens, Doyle, and Crook, *Search and Reflect*.
103. Jon Hendricks, ed., with Marianne Bech and Media Farzin, *Fluxus Scores and Instructions: The Transformative Years, "Make a Salad"* (Roskilde, Denmark: Museum for Contemporary Art, 2008); John Lely and James Saunders, *Word Events: Perspectives on Verbal Notation* (New York: Continuum, 2012); Robin Maconie, *Other Planets: The Complete Works of Karlheinz Stockhausen* (Lanham, MD: Rowman and Littlefield, 2016), 284–86, 304–6; Pauline Oliveros, *Anthology of Text Scores* (Kingston, NY: Deep Listening, 2013); Yoko Ono, *Grapefruit: A Book of Instruction* (London: Peter Owen, 1970).
104. Michael Nyman, *Experimental Music: Cage and Beyond*, 2nd ed. (Cambridge: Cambridge University Press, 1999), 72–88; Ono, *Grapefruit*.
105. Toop, *Into the Maelstrom*, 242–63.
106. Scott, *Noises*, 247–50.
107. Callingham, *Spontaneous Music*, 75–76.
108. Scott, *Noises*, 200, 246.
109. Scott, *Noises*, 54; Wickes, *Innovations in British Jazz*, 98.
110. Scott, *Noises*, 55–56.
111. Martin Davidson, liner notes to *Summer 1967*, by Spontaneous Music Ensemble, Emanem, 1996.
112. Stevens, Doyle, and Crook, *Search and Reflect*.
113. John Stevens and Martin Davidson, liner notes to *Face to Face*, by Spontaneous Music Ensemble, Emanem, 1995.

Chapter 5

1. Jones, *Blues People*, 225, 228; Jones, *Black Music*, 105, 107.
2. Jones, *Black Music*, 209.
3. Dixon, *L'Opera*, 86–87.
4. Jones, *Black Music*, 92–98.
5. Dixon, *L'Opera*, 15.
6. Bley, *Stopping Time*, 91–97; Benjamin Piekut, *Experimentalism Otherwise: The New York Avant-Garde and Its Limits* (Berkeley: University of California Press, 2011), 108–22, 127–39.
7. Christopher G. Bakriges, "Cultural Displacement, Cultural Creation: African-American Jazz Musicians in Europe from Bechet to Braxton," in *Cross*

the Water Blues: African American Music in Europe, ed. Neil A. Wynn (Jackson, MS: University Press of Mississippi, 2007), 250–65; Bakriges, *African American Musical Avant-Gardism*, 180–81.

8. Spellman, liner notes to *Ascension*; Spellman, *Four Lives in the Bebop Business*, 7–8; Wilmer, *As Serious as Your Life*, 46–47.

9. Spellman, *Four Lives in the Bebop Business*, 18–21.

10. Lewis, *A Power Stronger than Itself*, 243.

11. Whitney Balliett, "Jazz Concerts: Comes the Revolution," *New Yorker*, February 27, 1965, 121–24; Dan Morgenstern, "Caught in the Act," *Downbeat*, July 15, 1965, 12; Dan Morgenstern and Martin Williams, "The October Revolution: Two Views of the Avant Garde in Action," *Downbeat*, November 19, 1964, 15, 33; A. B. Spellman, "Jazz at the Judson," *Nation*, February 8, 1965, 149–51.

12. Dixon, *L'Opera*, 15; Bill Smith, "Archie Shepp: Four for Trane," *Coda*, October/November 1985, 21.

13. Litweiler, *Ornette Coleman*, 113; Ben Young, *Dixonia: A Bio-discography of Bill Dixon* (Westport, CT: Greenwood, 1998), 78.

14. Young, *Dixonia*, 339–67.

15. Anderson, *This Is Our Music*, 140–41.

16. Anderson, *This Is Our Music*, 130.

17. Kahn, *The House That Trane Built*, 5–11, 113–22, 131–40, 158–59, 173–74, 178–89.

18. Jason Weiss, *Always in Trouble: An Oral History of ESP-Disk, the Most Outrageous Record Label in America* (Middletown, CT: Wesleyan University Press, 2012), 20–22.

19. Weiss, *Always in Trouble*, 27–28.

20. Jones, *Black Music*, 128.

21. Young, *Dixonia*, 353.

22. Piekut, *Experimentalism Otherwise*, 135–36.

23. Kofsky, *Black Nationalism and the Revolution in Music*, 142–43; Young, *Dixonia*, 45.

24. Young, *Dixonia*, 348–50.

25. Ralph Berton, "Conversations with Bernard Stollman," *Sounds and Fury*, April 1966, 36–38; Weiss, *Always in Trouble*, 82, 104, 197.

26. Weiss, *Always in Trouble*, 26–27.

27. Anderson, *This Is Our Music*, 83.

28. Berton, "Conversations with Bernard Stollman"; Weiss, *Always in Trouble*, 27, 35–36.

29. Clifford Allen, "Bernard Stollman: The ESP-Disk Story," *All about Jazz*, November 21, 2005, http://www.allaboutjazz.com/php/article.php?id=19661; Piekut, *Experimentalism Otherwise*, 116–18; Weiss, *Always in Trouble*, 23.

30. Szwed, *Space Is the Place*, 152.

31. Szwed, *Space Is the Place*, 272–74.

32. Piekut, *Experimentalism Otherwise*, 107; Young, *Dixonia*, 362.

33. John Corbett, *Vinyl Freak: Love Letters to a Dying Medium* (Durham, NC: Duke University Press, 2017), 137–38; Jones, *Black Music*, 140.

34. Piekut, *Experimentalism Otherwise*, 122, 134; Eric Porter, *What Is This Thing Called Jazz? African American Musicians as Artists, Critics, and Activists* (Berkeley: University of California Press, 2002), 199; Marvin X, "From an Interview of Milford Graves," *Journal of Black Poetry* 1, no. 12 (1969): 46–55.

35. Archie Shepp, "An Artist Speaks Bluntly," *Downbeat*, December 16, 1965, 11.

36. Baraka, *The Autobiography of LeRoi Jones*, 298–99; Milford Graves, "Black Music: New Revolutionary Art," in *Black Arts: An Anthology of Black Creations*, ed. Ahmed Alhamisi (Detroit: Black Arts, 1969), 40; Jones, *Black Music*, 127; Woodard and Boehm, *The Black Power Movement*.

37. Janheinz Jahn, *Muntu: African Culture and the Western World* (New York: Grove, 1961), 124–27.

38. Loren Glass, *Counterculture Colophon: Grove Press, the Evergreen Review, and the Incorporation of the Avant-Garde* (Stanford, CA: Stanford University Press, 2012), 145–59.

39. Mathes, *Imagine the Sound*, 103–4.

40. Paul Ruppa, "Cecil Taylor and His Mendota Players: Snapshots," *Wire*, September 2020, https://www.thewire.co.uk/in-writing/essays/cecil-taylor-his-mendota-players-snapshots-by-paul-ruppa. The assigned reading is discussed in the comments section.

41. John Corbett, *Microgroove: Forays into Other Music* (Durham, NC: Duke University Press, 2015), 74–78; Mike Johnston, "Milford Graves: Master Drummer," *Coda*, November/December 1993, 6; Parker, *Conversations*, 41–44; Michael J. West, "Milford Graves, 1941–2021," *JazzTimes*, February 16, 2021, https://jazztimes.com/features/tributes-and-obituaries/milford-graves-1941-2021/.

42. Bivins, *Spirits Rejoice!*, 177–83; Milford Graves, "Book of Tono-rhythology," in *Arcana II: Musicians on Music*, ed. John Zorn (New York: Hips Road, 2007), 110–17; Milford Graves, "Music Extensions of Infinite Dimensions," in *Arcana V: Music, Magic, and Mysticism*, ed. John Zorn (New York: Hips Road, 2010), 171–86.

43. Isoardi, *The Dark Tree*, 49–51; Tapscott, *Songs of the Unsung*, 79–81.

44. Tapscott, *Songs of the Unsung*, 83.

45. Isoardi, *The Dark Tree*, 12–13.

46. Tapscott, *Songs of the Unsung*, 82–83.

47. Isoardi, *The Dark Tree*, 148–50.

48. Daniel Widener, *Black Arts West: Culture and Struggle in Postwar Los Angeles* (Durham, NC: Duke University Press, 2010), 119.

49. Isoardi, *The Dark Tree*, 95–98; Tapscott, *Songs of the Unsung*, 123–24.

50. Isoardi, *The Dark Tree*, 277.

51. Isoardi, *The Dark Tree*, 107–8, 111, 183–87; Tapscott, *Songs of the Unsung*, 147–48; Widener, *Black Arts West*, 134.

52. Isoardi, *The Dark Tree*, 183–87, 198–99, 239.
53. Tapscott, *Songs of the Unsung*, 126–30; Widener, *Black Arts West*, 130–31.
54. Isoardi, *The Dark Tree*, 103–4; Tapscott, *Songs of the Unsung*, 114–16.
55. Tapscott, *Songs of the Unsung*, 114.
56. Isoardi, *The Dark Tree*, 192–96; Tapscott, *Songs of the Unsung*, 175–78.
57. Lewis, *A Power Stronger than Itself* 96–99, 256–57.
58. Lock, *Forces in Motion*, 48.
59. Steinbeck, *Message to Our Folks*, 35–36, 55–59.
60. Lewis, *A Power Stronger than Itself*, 180.
61. Lewis, *A Power Stronger than Itself*, 111–14.
62. Lewis, *A Power Stronger than Itself*, 181.
63. Mike Johnston, "Chuck Nessa: Numbers One and Two," *Coda*, July/Aug 1992, 6.
64. Looker, *Point from Which Creation Begins*, 15–17.
65. Lewis, *A Power Stronger than Itself*, 268; Looker, *Point from Which Creation Begins*, 54–57.
66. Lewis, *A Power Stronger than Itself*, 271–73; Looker, *Point from Which Creation Begins*, 57, 130–32.
67. Looker, *Point from Which Creation Begins*, 189.
68. Looker, *Point from Which Creation Begins*, 88–90.
69. Scott, *Noises*, 259–60.
70. Callingham, *Spontaneous Music*, 22–23.
71. Scott, *Noises*, 265.
72. Scott, *Noises*, 279, 359.
73. Looker, *Point from Which Creation Begins*, 217–27.
74. Heller, *Loft Jazz*, 31–32; Jones, *Black Music*, 97.
75. Shoemaker, *Jazz in the Seventies*, 124–27.
76. Looker, *Point from Which Creation Begins*, 218–19.
77. Hermes, *Love Goes to Buildings on Fire*, 241.
78. Heller, *Loft Jazz*, 42–47; Shoemaker, *Jazz in the Seventies*, 134–35.
79. Heller, *Loft Jazz*, 83–86.
80. Heller, *Loft Jazz*, 35.
81. Heller, *Loft Jazz*, 94–95.
82. Bradley, *Universal Tonality*, 136; Joel Harrison, *Guitar Talk: Conversations with Visionary Players* (Newark, NJ: Terra Nova, 2021), 51; Heller, *Loft Jazz*, 33; Parker, *Conversations*, 368; Parker, *Conversations II*, 22–23, 219–20; William Parker, *Conversations III* (Paris: Rogueart, 2019), 40, 463–65; Radhika Philip, *Being Here: Conversations on Creating Music* (New York: Radhio.org, 2013), 96.
83. Lewis, *A Power Stronger than Itself*, 334–36, 578n35.
84. Lewis, *A Power Stronger than Itself*, 333–34.
85. Lewis, *A Power Stronger than Itself*, 336.

86. Shoemaker, *Jazz in the Seventies*, 144–52.
87. Heller, *Loft Jazz*, 50, 52; Looker, *Point from Which Creation Begins*, 241–42.
88. Looker, *Point from Which Creation Begins*, 241; Such, *Avant-Garde Jazz Musicians*, 85.
89. Nabil Ayers, "My Uncle's Jazz Shack," *New York Times*, August 12, 2018, MB1.
90. Such, *Avant-Garde Jazz Musicians*, 86.
91. Bakriges, "Cultural Displacement, Cultural Creation," 257; Heller, *Loft Jazz*, 56; Lewis, *A Power Stronger than Itself*, 344–49.
92. Heller, *Loft Jazz*, 100–119.
93. Heller, *Loft Jazz*, 28–29; Looker, *Point from Which Creation Begins*, 217–27.
94. Heller, *Loft Jazz*, 57–58; Looker, *Point from Which Creation Begins*, 240.
95. Heller, *Loft Jazz*, 125–26; Lewis, *A Power Stronger than Itself*, 331, 507–9; Teal, *Jazz Places*, 55–64.
96. Hermes, *Love Goes to Buildings on Fire*, x–xi.
97. Kyle Gann, *Music Downtown: Writings from the Village Voice* (Berkeley: University of California Press, 2006), xiii, 24; Hermes, *Love Goes to Buildings on Fire*, 45.
98. John Rockwell, "A New Music Director Comes to the Avant-Garde Kitchen," *New York Times*, September 14, 1980, D23.
99. Gann, *Music Downtown*, 1–15, 136–40; William Robin, *Industry: Bang on a Can and New Music in the Marketplace* (New York: Oxford University Press, 2021), 4–9.
100. Judy Chou, Mark Simon Haydn, Emmabeth Nanol, and Laura Schroffel, *The Kitchen Archive*, online finding aid, Getty Research Institute, 2017, https://www.getty.edu/research/special_collections/notable/the_kitchen.html; Lewis, *A Power Stronger than Itself*, 383.
101. Tom Johnson, *The Voice of New Music: New York City, 1972–1982* (Paris: Editions 75, 1989).
102. Lewis, *A Power Stronger than Itself*, 383–86; Rockwell, "A New Music Director," D23.
103. Anderson, *This Is Our Music*, 86, 141.
104. Bakriges, *African American Musical Avant-Gardism*, 25–28.
105. Spellman, *Four Lives in the Bebop Business*, 21.
106. Anderson, *This Is Our Music*, 176.
107. Anderson, *This Is Our Music*, 169; Bradley, *Universal Tonality*, 137.
108. Anderson, *This Is Our Music*, 172; Ed Hazell, "Sunrise Studio: All Music Is Greater than the Sum of Our Selves," *Point of Departure*, no. 41

(2012), https://www.pointofdeparture.org/PoD41/PoD41SunriseStudio2.html; Heller, *Loft Jazz*, 45.

109. Amy Beal, *Carla Bley* (Urbana: University of Illinois Press, 2011), 51–56; Allan Kozinn, "New-Music Record Distributor Is Closing," *New York Times*, June 12, 1990, C20; Robin, *Industry*, 193–94, 202.

110. Anderson, *This Is Our Music*, 171–72.

111. Lewis, *A Power Stronger than Itself*, 395, 401–2.

112. Anderson, *This Is Our Music*, 162–65.

113. Bakriges, "Cultural Displacement, Cultural Creation," 257.

Chapter 6

1. Vandermark, "Free Jazz, Genre and Style," 325–32.
2. Steinbeck, *Message to Our Folks*, 83–92
3. Steinbeck, *Message to Our Folks*, 92–106.
4. Steinbeck, *Message to Our Folks*, 76.
5. Kisiedu, *European Echoes*, 126.
6. Steinbeck, *Message to Our Folks*, 223.
7. Steinbeck, *Message to Our Folks*, 71.
8. Stephen H. Lehman, "I Love You with an Asterisk: African-American Experimental Music and the French Jazz Press, 1970–1980," *Critical Studies in Improvisation* 1, no. 2 (2005): 38–53, https://www.criticalimprov.com/article/view/18/49; Lewis, *A Power Stronger than Itself*, 240–44, 449; Lock, *Forces in Motion*, 82–83; Radano, *New Musical Figurations*, 25–27, 146–47, 266.
9. Steinbeck, *Message to Our Folks*, 223–25.
10. See also Eric Lewis, "What Is 'Great Black Music?' The Social Aesthetics of the AACM in Paris," in *Improvisation and Social Aesthetics*, ed. Georgina Born, Eric Lewis, and Will Straw (Durham, NC: Duke University Press, 2017), 135–59.
11. Steinbeck, *Message to Our Folks*, 225.
12. Alisha B. Wormsley, There Are Black People in the Future, https://www.thereareblackpeopleinthefuture.com/.
13. Steinbeck, *Message to Our Folks*, 250–58.
14. Steinbeck, *Message to Our Folks*, 209–10.
15. Looker, *Point from Which Creation Begins*, 147; Shoemaker, *Jazz in the Seventies*, 71.
16. Looker, *Point from Which Creation Begins*, 231.
17. Julius Hemphill, *The Music of Dogon A.D.: A Critical Edition*, ed. Marty Ehrlich (Verona, NJ: Subito Music, 2021).
18. Julius Hemphill, with Katea Stitt, *Julius Hemphill Interview*, 4 DAT audio cassettes and transcript, Jazz Oral History Project, Smithsonian Institution,

Washington, DC, 1995, https://sova.si.edu/details/NMAH.AC.0808; Ludwig Van Trikt, "Julius Hemphill Interview," *Cadence*, June 1995, 5–8.

19. Pascal James Imperato, "Contemporary Adapted Dances of the Dogon," *African Arts* 5, no. 1 (1971): 28–33, 68–72, 84.

20. Van Trikt, "Julius Hemphill Interview," 7.

21. Hemphill and Stitt, *Julius Hemphill Interview*.

22. Hemphill, *The Music of Dogon A.D.*

23. Hemphill and Stitt, *Julius Hemphill Interview*. See also James Clifford, *The Predicament of Culture: Twentieth-Century Ethnography, Literature, and Art* (Cambridge, MA: Harvard University Press, 1988), 55–91.

24. Shoemaker, *Jazz in the Seventies*, 68.

25. Joel Wanek and Tomeka Reid, "By Myself: An Interview with Abdul Wadud," *Point of Departure*, no. 57 (2016), https://www.pointofdeparture.org/PoD57/PoD57Wadud.html.

26. Hemphill, *The Music of Dogon A.D.*

27. "Hemphill: Rediscovering Julius Hemphill," Subito Music, accessed 2021, https://www.subitomusic.com/hemphill-rediscovering-julius-hemphill/; "Julius Hemphill (1938–1995): *The Boyé Multinational Crusade for Harmony* (Box Set)," New World Records, 2021, https://www.newworldrecords.org/collections/recent-release-3/products/julius-hemphill-1938-1995-the-boye-multi-national-crusade-for-harmony-box-set; Tamar Barzel, Marty Ehrlich, and Brian Fairley, *Julius Hemphill: Composer*, project website, https://wp.nyu.edu/library-hemphill_papers/.

Index

AACM (Association for the Advancement of Creative Musicians), 3, 73, 75, 79, 83, 84, 104–107, 109, 113, 115, 117–118
Abdul-Malik, Ahmed, 32–33
Abrams, Muhal Richard, 73, 84, 106, 108, 109, 113
Abstract Expressionism, 16, 59
Afrofuturism, 46, 118
Ali, Rashied, 37, 108–110
AMM, 62, 69
Art Ensemble of Chicago, 41–42, 75, 106, 111, 115–120
  "A Jackson in Your House," 8, 115–117, 119, 125
  "People in Sorrow," 119
Ayler, Albert, 54–57, 59, 61, 65, 66, 70, 93, 98, 99, 102, 116
  "Holy Ghost," 6, 51–52, 55–56
  Spiritual Unity, 52, 63, 99

BAG (Black Artists Group), 104–105, 107, 109–110, 112, 121
Bailey, Derek, 91, 93, 108
  non-idiomatic improvisation, 68–69
Bang, Billy, 57–58
Baraka, Amiri, 3, 5, 7, 45, 48, 51, 53, 54–56, 59–60, 95–96, 100, 102, 103, 108, 111
Barberi, Gato, 45–49

Beat movement in literature, 16
Bennink, Han, 62, 63, 66, 68
Berendt, Joachim-Ernst, 61–62
Berne, Tim, 124
Black Arts Repertory Theater/School, 56–58, 102, 112
Black, Jim, 124–125
Black Panthers, 40–41, 48, 57, 105
Blackwell, Ed, 17, 19, 46, 47
Bley, Carla, 8, 45, 97–98, 112–113
Bley, Paul, 2–3, 17, 19, 53–54, 76
  on ESP-Disk, 99–101
  in Jazz Composers Guild, 97–98
  with Sonny Rollins, 24–25, 27
Blue Note Records, 67, 98–99, 101
Bluiett, Hamiet, 104, 109, 120
Blythe, Arthur, 29, 109
Bowie, Lester, 41, 73, 107, 109, 116–118
Bradford, Bobby, 34
Braxton, Anthony, 28, 29, 69, 76–82, 89, 104, 106, 109, 111, 113, 118
  Composition 4, 77
  Composition 6C, 77
  Composition 6F, 77
  Composition 10, 77
  Composition 18, 77
  Composition 23C, 77
  Composition 23G, 80
  Composition 40M, 77

153

Braxton, Anthony *(continued)*
  Composition 58, 77–78
  Composition 59, 78
  Composition 69Q, 78
  Composition 76, 4, 78
  Composition 77H, 80
  Compositions 108A–D, 80
  Composition 114, 78
  Composition 115, 78
  Ghost Trance Music, 81–82, 89
  9 Compositions (Iridium) 2006, 81, 89
  Three Compositions of New Jazz, 73, 75
Breuker, Willem, 64, 68
Brötzmann, Peter, 60–66, 68
  For Adolphe Sax, 63, 66, 67, 70
  Machine Gun, 60, 63–65
Brown, Marion, 28, 57, 58, 74–75, 99, 109, 110, 123
Brubeck, Dave, 12
Bryant, Dave, 23
Burrell, Dave, 40–41, 109
BYG Actuel, 41, 47, 107, 115

Cage, John, 14, 92, 106, 111–112
Carroll, Baikida, 109, 120, 122
Carter, John, 28
Cherry, Don, 8, 26, 47, 64, 98, 108, 111
  with Ornette Coleman, 15, 17, 18, 20, 21, 23, 58
  with Sonny Rollins, 26, 96
Cline, Alex, 8–9, 119
Cline, Nels, 8–9, 65, 122
Coleman, Denardo, 29, 63
Coleman, Ornette, 1, 6, 14–30, 45, 63, 66, 76, 78, 84, 91, 96, 98, 99, 108, 112, 113, 115, 123–124
  "Chronology," 18
  The Empty Foxhole, 29–30
  "Free," 20

Free Jazz, 3, 20, 58, 64
"Lonely Woman," 17–18
Skies of America, 21–22, 81
Coltrane, Alice, 6, 37–39, 43, 44–45, 56, 99
Coltrane, John, 6, 7, 26, 31–40, 42–44, 48–49, 56–60, 79, 84, 93, 95–99, 101, 115, 117
  "Alabama," 34–35
  Ascension, 51, 58–60, 64, 97
  "Giant Steps," 12–13, 19
  "India," 32–33
  A Love Supreme, 35–36, 43
  "My Favorite Things," 31–33
  "Ogunde," 56
  Om, 36–37, 67
  Saint John Will-I-Am Coltrane African Orthodox Church, 43
  "Spiritual," 34
Connors, Norman, 46–47, 49, 67–69
Cooper-Moore, 55, 109
Corea, Chick, 27, 40, 46
Crispell, Marilyn, 3, 55, 80–81
Crouch, Stanley, 4, 108, 109
Cyrille, Andrew, 41, 109

D'Angelo, Andrew, 125
Davis, Miles, 30, 31–33, 53, 117
  electric music, 27–28, 46–48
  Kind of Blue, 11–12
  Second Great Quintet, 6, 27–28, 123
Dixon, Bill, 3, 28, 96–98, 100, 112, 113
Dolphy, Eric, 27, 53, 58, 91, 98
  with Ornette Coleman, 58
  with John Coltrane, 32, 38
  with Charles Mingus, 26
Downbeat magazine, 30, 35, 57, 98, 102, 106, 108, 111, 112

Edwards, Marc, 55

Ehrlich, Marty, 122, 124
Ellman, Liberty, 84–85
ESP-Disk, 99–101, 107
Evans, Bill, 11, 12, 13–14, 25, 123

Favors, Malachi, 41–42, 116, 117
Fell, Simon H., 69

Giuffre, Jimmy, 14, 26
Gomez, Eddie, 13, 40
Graves, Milford, 40, 53, 66, 99, 108, 113
Live at Yale University/Nommo, 101–104
Greene, Burton, 97–98, 100, 109
Grimes, Henry, 2, 26
Gustafsson, Mats, 65
Guy, Barry, 52, 69–70, 108

Haden, Charlie, 28, 45, 123–124
Liberation Music Orchestra, 45
with Ornette Coleman, 15, 17–21
Halvorson, Mary, 81, 113
Hancock, Herbie, 27, 46, 47, 98, 117
Harris, Beaver, 45
Hemphill, Julius, 109, 110, 111
"Dogon A.D" 8–9, 120–125
Higgins, Billy, 17, 26
Holland, Dave, 27, 28, 68, 91
Hubbard, Freddie, 30, 58, 98
Human Arts Ensemble, 107, 111

Impulse Records, 99–101
Iyer, Vijay, 9, 113, 123

Jahn, Janheinz, 102–103, 120
Jarman, Joseph, 73, 116–117
Jarrett, Keith, 6, 25, 28, 124
Jazz Composers Guild, 96–102, 109, 112
Jenkins, Leroy, 73, 75
Joans, Ted, 40–41, 59

Jones, Elvin, 31, 33, 36–37, 48
Jones, LeRoi, *see* Baraka, Amiri
Jost, Ekkehard, 18, 22, 52, 68, 72

King, Martin Luther, Jr., 34, 36
Kofsky, Frank, 57, 102
Kowald, Peter, 7, 60–63, 66, 67

Lacy, Steve, 19, 69, 98, 113
LaFaro, Scott, 13, 25
Lake, Oliver, 103, 109, 111
Laswell, Bill, 65, 110
Lateef, Yusef, 40, 43, 88
Lawrence, Azar, 48–49
Lee, Don L., 40–41
Lee, Jeanne, 41, 111
Lewis, George, 3–4, 69, 109, 111–114
Liebig, Steuart, 8–9, 122
Logan, Giuseppi, 57, 99, 101
Lowe, Frank, 57
Lyons, Jimmy, 28, 71–72, 109, 110
Lytton, Paul, 69–70

Manne, Shelly, 3, 15, 30
Mantler, Michael, 97–98, 112–113
Marsalis, Branford, 28–29
Marsalis, Wynton, 28–29, 110
McBee, Cecil, 46, 67–69
MC5, 65
Metheny, Pat, 25, 28
Mingus, Charles, 2, 12, 35, 98, 101, 104, 117
Charles Mingus Presents Charles Mingus, 26, 42
Mitchell, Nicole, 81, 114, 118
Mitchell, Roscoe, 41, 73, 109, 116, 118–119, 123
"Solo," 74
Moncur, Grachan, III, 27, 40–41, 57, 98
"New Africa," 41
Morgan, Lee, 30, 34, 101

Morris, Lawrence "Butch," 85–88, 90
Motian, Paul, 13, 25, 28, 53
Mtume [James Mtume Forman], 46–49
Murray, David, 2, 85–86, 104, 108–110
Murray, Sunny, 40–42, 52–55, 57, 61, 66
  with Albert Ayler, 6–7, 54, 55, 99
  with Cecil Taylor, 52–53, 67
Musica Elettronica Viva, 69, 77

Nation of Islam, 56, 105
National Endowment for the Arts, 105–106, 110, 112
Neal, Larry, 51, 103, 113
Negritude movement, 41, 103
New York Art Quartet, 57, 98, 99, 101

Olatunji, Babatunde, 39–40, 42, 43
Ono, Yoko, 93, 111
Oxley, Tony, 62

Paik, Naim June, 93
Parker, Evan, 68–70, 107–108
  with Peter Brötzmann, 63–64, 68
  with Spontaneous Music Ensemble, 91–94
Parker, William, 89–90
Peacock, Gary
  with Albert Ayler, 52, 54–55, 99
  with Bill Evans, 13, 24–25
Portal, Michel, 61, 66
Pullen, Don, 101–104

Redman, Dewey, 28, 123–124
Rivers, Sam, 7, 28, 98
  with Cecil Taylor, 67, 72
  Streams, 46, 67–69
  Studio Rivbea, 108–110

Roach, Max, 39–40, 98, 101
Rollins, Sonny, 7
  Our Man in Jazz, 26, 95–96
  Sonny Rollins Meets Coleman Hawkins, 2, 24–25, 27
ROVA Saxophone Quartet, 90–91
Rowe, Keith, 4, 62
Rudd, Roswell, 45, 97–98
Rudolph, Adam, 87–88
Russell, George, 25–26
Rutherford, Paul, 68–69, 91, 108
Rzewski, Frederic, 77

Sanders, Pharoah, 6, 37, 40, 42–47, 57, 65, 99
  with Alice Coltrane, 38
  with John Coltrane, 36–38, 56, 58
  "The Creator Has a Master Plan," 42–44, 46–47
Santana, Carlos, 44
Schlippenbach, Alexander von, 60, 63, 68
Schoof, Manfred, 60, 63, 68
Schuller, Gunther, 2–3, 12, 15–16
Sharp, Elliott, 65, 110
Shepp, Archie, 8, 28, 45, 55, 57, 102, 111, 113
  Four for Trane, 99–100
  in Jazz Composers Guild, 98–100
  on John Coltrane *Ascension*, 51, 58–59
  Live at the Pan-African Festival, 40–41
  The Magic of Ju-Ju, 46
  "Mama Too Tight," 2, 45
  "Touareg," 41–42
  "Yasmina, a Black Woman," 41–42
Silva, Alan, 40–41, 64
Smith, Lonnie Liston, 45

Smith, Wadada Leo, 73–76, 83, 97, 109, 111
"The Bell," 4, 75
"Nine (9) Stones on Mountain," 74
"Silence," 75
Sonic Youth, 65
Sorey, Tyshawn, 85, 113, 123–124
Speed, Chris, 124–125
Spellman, A. B., 51, 57, 59, 97, 112, 113
Stevens, John, 91–94, 108
Stockhausen, Karlheinz, 69, 79–80, 92
Sun Ra, 51, 57, 59–60, 64, 65, 100, 105, 113, 115
Atlantis, 40
Cosmic Tones for Mental Therapy, 86
conducted improvisations, 86
El Saturn Research, 101–102
"India," 38–39
in Jazz Composers Guild, 96–100
The Nubians of Plutonia, 39

Tagaki, Mototeru, 66, 119
Takayanagi, Masayuki, 66
Tapscott, Horace, 48, 86, 105–106
Taylor, Cecil, 51, 52, 67, 70–72, 84, 103, 104, 111, 112, 113, 115
in Jazz Composers Guild, 96–99
Love for Sale, 13
Unit Structures, 71, 98
Tchicai, John, 58, 97–98
Thompson, Walter, 87

Thomas, Leon, 43–44
Thornton, Clifford, 40–41
Threadgill, Henry, 83–85, 107, 109, 113, 123
"See the Blackbird Now," 85
"Spotted Dick is Pudding," 83
Togashi, Masahiko, 66, 67, 119
Towner, Ralph, 25

UGMAA (Union of God's Musicians and Artists Ascension), 104–107, 109
US Organization, 47, 48, 105

Vandermark, Ken, 4, 115
Wadud, Abdul, 120–123
Ware, David S., 55, 109
Watts, Trevor, 91, 93, 94, 108
Wessel, Kenny, 23–24
Weston, Randy, 34, 39, 109–110
Whitaker, Harry, 49
Williams, Buster, 27, 47, 49
Williams, Tony, 27, 53, 98, 117
Wilson, Philip, 120–122
Wright, Frank, 63, 70

X, Malcolm, 56, 57, 103

Yoshizawa, Motoharu, 66
Young, LaMonte, 4, 93, 111

Zorn, John, 4, 65, 90, 110, 111
"Cobra," 88–89

www.ingramcontent.com/pod-product-compliance
Lightning Source LLC
Chambersburg PA
CBHW031402230426
43670CB00006B/622